Running with Stilettos

Running with Stilettos

✦

Living a Balanced Life in Dangerous Shoes

Mary T. Wagner

iUniverse, Inc.
New York   Bloomington

Running with Stilettos
Living a Balanced Life in Dangerous Shoes

iUniverse books may be ordered through booksellers or by contacting:

iUniverse
1663 Liberty Drive
Bloomington, IN 47403
www.iuniverse.com
1-800-Authors (1-800-288-4677)

Because of the dynamic nature of the Internet, any Web addresses or links contained in this book may have changed since publication and may no longer be valid. The views expressed in this work are solely those of the author and do not necessarily reflect the views of the publisher, and the publisher hereby disclaims any responsibility for them.

ISBN: 978-0-595-49242-8 (pbk)
ISBN: 978-0-595-61023-5 (ebk)

Printed in the United States of America

First edition published March, 2008
Second edition published December, 2008

iUniverse rev. date: 12/10/2008

This leap of faith is dedicated to …

my children—Deborah, Sarah, Michael and Robert—

for the joy of your existence, your love, your laughter, and your fearless example.

and to Chuck … for the lightness and music in my heart.

Contents

Foreword ix

Chain Reaction 1

Chocolate Sobriety 5

Back seat…rider 10

The Devil on Horseback 13

Girls in the Graveyard 17

Cordless and Dangerous 20

The Tale of the Christmas Axes 26

End of the taxi line 29

The Island 32

Wildflower seeds and beer 36

The Carpe Diem girls 41

Of Shoes and Strategy 46

Ripple Effect 49

Gone Fishin' 52

Cookie Therapy 56

Bunny Blues 60

Spellbound in Hibernia 63

The Gatorade Reality Check 66

A Tale of Two Kitties 69

Return to the Fatherland 72

The Closets of Doom 77

Life with Predators 81

End of the Trail 85

Law & Disorder 88

Turbo Dating—a year in review 91

A Little Clutter Please! 97

Love in Wood and Wax 100

On the road again 103

Thelma and Louise on spring break 106

Emergency Makeup Kit 112

Ghosts in the Pasture 114

About the Author...117

Foreword

I bought my first set of stilettos not when I was a lithe and lissome young twenty-something, but when I was ... oh, never mind. The fresh-faced and skinny days as a journalism student in college had been lived quite naturally in jeans and sneakers. Marriage and motherhood followed closely on the heels of my graduation and brand-new career as a newspaper reporter. And as every mother knows, rounding up energetic toddlers is a lot like herding cats. You have the best chance of success when you're in running shoes.

Even law school and then a job as a prosecutor didn't reverse the sartorial tide. I'd already gotten too used to comfort in the interval, conducting transatlantic phone interviews as a freelance writer in my shorts and bare feet and occasionally my pajamas, taking the kids to the beach in flip-flops, racing through the grocery store and leading Brownie troops through adventures in the woods in scuffed Reeboks. Sensible shoes did just fine.

The turning point came, as they usually do, during a time of high stress. One of my brood had a mysterious health crisis, and I was killing time between driving her around campus by reading cases in a overstuffed chair by the fireside at Starbucks. Ever the multi-tasker, I was researching drunk driving law for an upcoming argument in court when I had one of those "eureka" moments that Archimedes made famous. Unlike Archimedes, I didn't then get up and run wet and naked out into the street. My uniquely personal response was to stash the photocopied cases, notebooks, pens and yellow highlighters back in the tote bag and go shoe shopping. I said I was "sensible." I didn't say I was dead!

I picked a mall on the west side of Madison, and went looking for brown shoes. Well "brown" can cover a lot of plain and uninspired ground. But for some whimsical reason I decided to try on, in the midst of all the utilitarian shoes I was looking at, a drop-dead dangerous pair of faux brown alligator sling-back heels with three inch ice-pick spikes. They looked great. I was timid, and asked the salesperson to put them on "hold." I picked my daughter up from class and brought her back to the mall with me. It took her about five seconds to size me up as I teetered, and then she delivered a verdict. "Mom, those are really cute. You should buy them." She'd been voted "best dressed" two or three times at her high school. Who was I to argue?

The alligator spikes came home with me and I wore them to work the next day. Another attorney in the courthouse who happened to be male and who shall forever mercifully remain nameless took one look at them, laughed self-consciously, and said "My God, Mary, those are the sexiest shoes I've ever seen!" And I immediately realized two things. One was "*hey, I think I'm on to something here!*" And the other was, "*oh, I am gonna have me some FUN!*"

That was a good two dozen pairs ago. Smooth leather, suede, brocade, snakeskin, pink fake-alligator, plaid, tweed, spectators, cutouts, sling-backs, stacked heels, wood heels, curved heels, bows, they've all been singing my song at some point. Most have made it into a courtroom at one time or another. And yes, they've certainly been fun.

If there's a broader lesson to be learned from this eleventh-hour style conversion, its simply that it's never too late to take a few chances, pick up a new vice, find some new and unaffected joy, and of vital importance, simply open your eyes and your heart to things you just never thought or imagined you'd do.

And if you can keep from breaking an ankle in the process, so much the better …

Chain Reaction

You can look at it finally abandoning the last of the feminine "rescue" fantasies. Or maybe it was just a dose of latent pioneer spirit finally coming to the surface. Though Davy Crockett never had one of these. (Of course, Davy Crockett never had a pair of leopard-print stilettos in his closet either. Or so we hope.)

Either way, I bought a chain saw.

My favorite dead tree came down last week in a thunderstorm that swept through with brief and sudden fury while I was standing in the video section of Pick 'n' Save looking for a copy of the chick flick, "Ever After." Not getting drenched as I dashed to the car—or alternatively, swept off to Oz or maybe just the next county—was the only thing on my mind as I made a run for it through the sheets of water flying sideways through the parking lot.

Then I rounded the last of the curve in the driveway, and hit the brakes, fast. High beams illuminated a swath of splintered dead wood spread across the concrete, making the last fifty feet to the garage completely impassable. Bark and branches were scattered everywhere, the trunk split and broken into huge chunks. I'd have my work cut out for me the next morning. I drove my itty-bitty Honda delicately around the carnage on the grass next to the flower beds, and put the car away. I went to sleep pondering my options.

As dead trees stood, I hated to see this one go. It had died several years earlier from unknown causes, along with a dozen or more in the same stretch of the front acres. I spent the last few winters wondering

1

just when this one would either come down on one of the cars, or just drop across the drive moments before we had to leave for work or school. But where most visitors surveyed its precarious placement and said "that's gotta come down before it falls on something!," I looked at it and wistfully countered, "maybe another year?"

Perched just feet from the edge of the drive, this tree came to provide more amusement dead than alive. Woodpeckers had drilled holes in the trunk, and they nested there last summer. I found this out when I searched for the source of incredible chattering nearby in the mornings while I was trying to catch a little more sleep. Living out in the country, the birds are never silent in the morning. But this took nature's alarm clock to a whole new decibel level.

Process of elimination led me to the dead tree, and so I stationed myself in front of it and waited. And waited. Minutes passed, and nothing happened. Finally, there was movement in the shadow of one of the holes. A fluffy, black-and-white head with a pointy beak popped up long enough to get a bead on me, then vanished again. Downy woodpeckers, for years frequent visitors to my backyard feeder. Catching a glimpse of them in the hole-ridden snag became a daily game for me, sort of a "Wild America" version of the arcade game "whack-amole." But now the next set of nesting woodpeckers would just have to live elsewhere.

The tree had shattered when it hit the pavement, and I separated most of the giant tangle of wood and bark by just finding the fracture lines and then snapping the branches in the other direction and dragging them out of the way. A pile of dead wood grew in the back yard, promising a blaze of glory like a Viking funeral pyre when I finally set a match to it. The driveway eventually cleared, but huge twisted branches and shattered trunks still lay across the lawn, like naked corpses waiting for burial.

Hmmmmm … what to do? Wait a month for the-boyfriend-with-chainsaw to get done with his own voluminous yard work and finally cut me some firewood? Break out my handsaw and try to do it the old fashioned way? My shoulders and neck still ached from the rudimentary clean-up job I'd already done. It might finally be time to go window shopping.

I'd been in the same position a couple of years earlier. Stumbling across fallen branches on the snowy footpath in the dark one evening on my way to admire the deer my son had just brought down nearby, I knew that snowshoeing was going to be a deathtrap if I didn't clear the trail soon. I took myself to Menards the next morning, and reluctantly perused the chain saw section.

They looked big. They looked dangerous. They looked heavy, and menacing, and manly, and hard to handle. They looked like an invitation to gasoline-powered amputation. I furrowed my brow and paced back and forth. "Can I help you, ma'am?" A polite young man in a blue apron stood ready to assist. I wasn't going to be easy to please.

"Do you have anything smaller?" I asked, already knowing the answer. Did these come in anything like a 'Lady Remington' version? Something stamped "SAFETY" all over it, suitable for the Sesame Street set? Something that could guarantee that I wouldn't cut off a limb? Something specifically built for the female customer, and you know, it would look just great in pink?

"Maybe you'd be more comfortable with a hand saw," he suggested, and that's what I eventually walked through the checkout line with. It worked fine—and gave my back and arms a good workout to boot— for just about every woodcutting project I had until now.

I made my way back to Menards. Stopped at Starbucks first on this glorious and sunny day for a tall mocha frappucino with "half the whip." A girl's got to start the day right. And caffeine gives you courage. I walked through the front door of the store with no more enthusiasm than I'd had the last time. Even less, in fact. I've **seen** that episode of "CSI" where the bloody homicide scene is eventually solved by the revelation that some idiot didn't know how to handle his own chainsaw and killed himself by accident.

I found the death and dismemberment row … oops, the chainsaw section. Made my way down the aisle once more, noting that the main distinguishing feature of all these was that some were powered by small gasoline motors (eewwww … the smell!), and others operated with an electric cord. Yes, I could foresee much in the way of disaster from tripping over the cord the same way you trip over the cord to the living room lamp.

And then I saw it. Nearly overlooked it in my gloom, and in the shadows cast by its larger cousins. Sitting at eye level, but chain facing away from me, like a puppy burrowed into a pile of blankets, was … the answer. Since the last time I went looking, Black & Decker had made a cordless chain saw. I stared in amazement. It was tiny, weighing barely six pounds. I picked it up. I have kitchen appliances that are bigger. It was rechargeable. The "bar" was only eight inches long. It looked like two bigger chain saws had had a baby. My breadmaker came in a bigger box. Despite the color scheme—a utiltarian, no, let's be honest, ugly—black and orange, it was actually CUTE.

It seemed like a perfect fit. I bought it, of course. I like being rescued just as much as the next girl, but I confess that my favorite scene in "Ever After" comes at the very end when Drew Barrymore, the beleaguered Cinderella of the story, manages to turn the tables on her odious captor and frees herself at sword point. It takes her handsome prince a bit by surprise when he gallantly shows up late for the rescue, but they gamely set out to live happily ever after anyway.

I suspect that when winter comes and I throw the first log on the fire that I've actually cut from a real tree myself, it's going to be a very interesting moment. Definitely one to mark with a celebratory toast. In the meantime, I'm just enjoying owning my newest toy.

Now if only it came in pink …

Chocolate Sobriety

I made it forty-five days once. Forty five days of grasping, white-knuckle determination, of denial, of yearning, of walking past the siren call of an unfinished Kit Kat on the kitchen table, of reaching for a pretzel instead of another Hershey Kiss.

Chocolate sobriety ain't for the faint of heart. The forty-five day stretch was a benchmark more than a dozen years ago that hasn't been equaled since. Though I tried it again earlier this year, thought once more that even if I started not that long before the national chocolate holiday of Easter, I could hold my breath and tough it out. I should have known better. I made it nineteen days this time, each day of denial meticulously marked off on a three-by-five card stuck to the refrigerator door, each day a badge of pride and punishment and self-control. I got derailed, not by the Easter Bunny this time, but by my cousin Ann in Ireland, when she cheerfully welcomed me and my son to her lovely kitchen overlooking the Atlantic Ocean by opening a box of Irish chocolate-covered biscuits. When in Rome, do as the Romans do. When in Dunmore East … well, the chocolate always DOES taste better in Europe.

Yes, we're talking hard-core addiction here. Whatever chocolate cake happens to be in the refrigerator left-over from a birthday celebration is of course breakfast du jour with a cup of tea, whether it's my sour-cream chocolate layer cake with buttercream frosting, chocolate covered mint squares, death-by-chocolate brownies, or chocolate amaretto cheesecake. I can eat chocolate for breakfast, lunch, dinner, and mid-day snacks. And frequently do. While I raid the candy bowl at work on a daily basis, I also keep a stash of Dove chocolates in a co-worker's file cabinet in his office down the hall. My theory is that if I keep them in my office they'll be gone in a few hours, but if they're in his, I'll be too embarrassed to make more than one or two raids a day. Some days it even works.

I knew I was in serious addiction territory many years ago when I read a lengthy and serious article about alcoholism, went through the checklist that accompanied the article and realized that you could substitute "chocolate" for the word "alcohol" in each of the dozen red-flag questions designed to getting you to run for your life toward a recovery group.

And yes, I've heard the joke. "Why are there no twelve-step programs for chocoholics?" "Because nobody wants to quit."

Not that I don't want to, for a lot of good reasons. The extra pounds I'm carrying in my caboose, for one. All the cravings and the mood swings and blood sugar spikes and crashes for another. You can tell me all you want about new medical findings that dark chocolate is actually good for your health in any number of ways. (And yes, in fact, my cholesterol level is admirably, remarkably healthy, as is my blood pressure.) The fact of the matter is, I've been good and hooked since I was a little girl and my mother started me off on Hershey Kisses as treats on the theory that all other candies containing artificial food colorings were bad. And addiction is never a good thing. Chocolate is my comfort food, my "brain food" when I'm on a heavy thinking deadline, my preferred dessert, my ultimate self-indulgence. Give up sex or chocolate? Hmmmmmm … Gotta think about that one for a minute.

I still look back at that forty-five day stretch with longing, and pride, and ultimately disappointment. And I remember exactly what tipped me back off the wagon.

I'd taken four kids down to Chicago for a family visit around Easter time. Four kids aged eleven down through through one-and-a half. Suitcases, collapsible stroller, diaper bag, snacks, toys, books. It was like packing to emigrate. And we crammed a lot into a day that didn't go nearly as smoothly in real life as it had in the planning stages.

We shoe-horned my Aunt Mary into the minivan with us that morning and took off to visit the Museum of Science and Industry on the city's far south side. Got there and found that the exhibit she meant us to see wasn't available. Drove back toward the city and decided to hit the Field Museum of Natural History at the south end of the Loop instead. Parked in another zip code because of parking lot renovations around the museum. Waited for about a half hour in line to get our lunches at the crowded McDonald's in the basement of the museum. Holiday cheer with your fries, anyone? Rescheduled seeing a college pal until later in the day because of all the hitches in meandering so far. Tried to beat the rush hour traffic on the Kennedy Expressway by taking the side roads out from the Loop. Got snarled up instead in the traffic jam surrounding Wrigley Field for NBA star Michael Jordan's professional baseball debut in an exhibition game between the White Sox and the Chicago Cubs. April 7, 1994. A day that will live in infamy, both for professional baseball and me.

We dragged ourselves back into the house, lugged the kids and all their gear up to my aunt's second story apartment where we planned to settle in. She reached behind the pictures on the fireplace mantle, took out some Easter treats for the kids she'd hidden behind them. Fannie May chocolate, the holy grail of self-indulgence. I'd spent a college summer working in the Loop, never packing a lunch, making a three-day circuit between Fannie May, Baskin Robbins and Heinemann's bakery. She'd bought each kid a bag of Fannie May chocolate eggs and a Fannie May chocolate bunny, and started handing them out.

"Gee, Mary Therese, it's such a shame that now's the time you've decided to give up eating chocolate." It wasn't a taunt, just an observation, but I felt something inside me tip. I looked down at Robert who was not quite two, and realized he would have no memory of this moment. I turned to my aunt, and ordered, "Give me that bunny." It was gone in seconds.

That was the high point on the chocolate sobriety meter, or the low point, however you look at it. Though addiction has just now shown its better side.

I had some surgery done on an outpatient basis not long ago, and my friend Judy came out to the hospital to babysit me there and then take me home later. Blessed with both a nursing degree, a wicked sense of humor, and friendship of more than three decades, she came fully equipped with an apple ("an apple a day keeps the doctor away!"), a box of Garfield decorated bandages, a gardening magazine, a box of chocolate-dipped devil's food donuts for my breakfast the next day, a bag of Dove dark chocolate miniatures, and a bag of Ghirardelli 60% cacao dark chocolate squares. Chocolate of thoroughly medicinal strength if you believe the scientific research these days. Not on the hospital menu, but still assuredly very, very good for you.

The operation went off without a hitch, though with the combination of a short stretch under general anesthetic and then a shot of morphine for pain later, I was pretty out of it for a while. Still, after a half hour of chewing on the ice chips Judy was spoon-feeding me, I was starting to feel restless and ready to leave.

The thing about hospitals and nurses though, is, there are certain benchmarks they want you to hit before they let you out the door with their blessing and a sheet of instructions in six point type. Chewing ice chips is one. Not falling over when you get up is another. And proving that you can eat something without throwing it back up a minute later is another key test. Okay, I played ball. "I want some sherbet."

The order went out into the hospital universe somewhere. She wants sherbet, not soup, not sandwiches, not cheesecake. More ice chips followed, along with an unassisted trip to the bathroom (another benchmark, yea!), some sips of water, and the question, "where's my sherbet?" Somewhere in transit. I settled in yet again, watched the clock, watched Dr. Phil, ate some more ice chips, got dressed in my street clothes. Still no sherbet.

It appeared the hospital had had to dispatch someone from the kitchen to go to the Himalayas to shoot the elusive Tibetan sherbet yak, and preparation was still going to take a while. Time to take matters into our own hands. "Judy, I think it's time we broke into the chocolate you smuggled in."

We hit the Ghirardelli first, then the Dove. I kept it all down, though it was a little hard getting it down my throat in the first place because of the "cotton mouth" effect of the anesthesia. Still, it was enough to impress the powers that be, and after signing the paperwork they popped me into a wheelchair and pushed me out to Judy's car waiting at the curb.

I finally dug into the sherbet as I was going through the sliding doors, finished it as we were driving down the street to my house. Score one for my demons.

Back seat...rider

In all honesty, I was praying for rain. Looked out my office window wistfully, at the little patch of sky not completely blocked off by the building across the alley from the courthouse. A bit overcast, a chance of showers. Another look an hour later. Clear skies and sunshine again.

Damn my luck!

Dinner was in the offing, my treat, a thank you and a reward for the hours of sweat and backbreaking labor and music and laughter that had gone into converting a good 300 square feet of gravel and plastic sheeting around my house into an oasis of blooming, bursting flowers and greenery, accented with Arizona sandstone flagstones the color of a desert sunset. And if the weather cooperated, he was going to leave the pickup truck behind and finally bring the bike.

There are consequences to dating a guy with a Harley. Yes, there's the whole mystique ... the gleaming chrome, the marvelous, primal thump of the engine, the shades and stubble, the black leather pants. But at some point, it's not just window dressing, not something you stand next to and hope it doesn't outshine your outfit. At some point, he's going to want you on the back of the bike with him. And my day of reckoning had finally arrived.

Still, I dressed for a different occasion, hoping that some shred of caution—check the weather, thunderstorms possible later!—would keep the bike in the garage and our transport involving four wheels and a roof. Blue plaid capri pants. Fluttery white see-through shirt over a skinny white tank top. Sandals and bare ankles.

The man and the Harley arrived on time, the bike gleaming in the sunlight, the man grinning and triumphant with anticipation. We sat on lawn chairs in the yard for a while, admiring the new and improved landscape, and I catalogued all the drawbacks I could think of.

I have trust issues. I'll be the first to admit I'm a control freak. And I play by the rules, virtually all of the time. I never go in the "Exit" door at Wal-Mart, even when it's closer and it's standing wide open. Speed scares me to death, unless I'm the one driving. I'm terrified of heights, and I have absolutely no sense of balance. Stiletto heels are all the altitude I need. I like traveling in cars. Especially cars with air conditioning, and CD players, and cup holders for my Starbucks, and air bags, oh yes, with air bags.

He listened patiently, then once again eloquently described his love of riding on that doggone motorcycle. The freedom. The sensation of the wind on your skin and all of nature around you. The magnificent sound. And he promised to keep to the speed limit. Then he reached into a storage compartment and thoughtfully brought out a spare helmet and his good black leather jacket. I tried it on. With the plaid capri pants and sandals, I looked ridiculous. I exited stage left, and returned more suitably attired. Dark jeans, black high-heeled boots. I ditched the foofy white shirt in favor of something snug and knit. Shrugged into the jacket, put on the helmet, got on the back seat. In truth, the battle had been lost before it was even joined. Then with a couple of basic instructions—lean into the turns with him or stay neutral instead of leaning the other way, loosen my death grip just a little so he could both breathe and drive—we took off slowly down the driveway and made it safely and without fanfare or hysteria to the restaurant three miles away.

That was a few hundred miles ago, and there are countless more on the agenda. I may start shopping for my own helmet. But I like borrowing the jacket, something so chivalrous and gallant about that gesture that makes me feel protected in ways that have nothing to do with how much leather stands between me and the pavement.

I used to think that sex was the final frontier in human intimacy, measured in hushed and sacred increments of trust, and closeness, and sharing, and vulnerability. I was wrong. You can make a whole lot of whoopee and still hold much of yourself back, hide those private places you don't want to share, feel like you're still somehow in control. The much bigger leap of raw faith and reliance is getting on the back of a motorcycle, wrapping your arms around someone's waist, and with a touch wordlessly conveying, "here's my life, I'm trusting you to keep me safe."

Scary, and terrifying, and thrilling, and totally liberating all in one. And yes, to my great surprise, I've found I really like the view from the back seat.

The Devil on Horseback

The price of admission to my own mind cost less than a Godiva chocolate bar at Barnes & Noble.

The Indian summer sun beat down brightly on my bare shoulders as I picked my leisurely way through a massive flea market beside the Mississippi River in Iowa with my daughters. We were giddy fugitives from routine on that rare weekend together, and meandering and winnowing and pointing things out proved to be a bottomless well of amusement.

Hey, look at those Saint Bernard puppies lounging over there in the shade! Get a load of the cute Halloween yard decorations! What do think this weird metal utensil was used for fifty years ago? Whaddaya think, should I buy this?

We turned over crockery and porcelain teacups, priced knick-knacks, pored over collections of used CDs, sniffed fragrant soaps, eyeballed cheap jewelry. And as I casually glanced at a box of second hand books, the past nearly bit me on the finger.

There, atop a stack of other scuffed and unmemorable books, was the key to my formative years: a "romantic suspense" novel by Victoria Holt, called "The Devil on Horseback." The original paper dustcover was still intact, though faded. Center stage was occupied by a wasp-waisted young, beautiful blond with long ringlets trailing from beneath a feathered blue bonnet the size of a Volkswagen Beetle. She was flanked by images of a booted, sneering nobleman (in a smaller but just as ridiculous feathered hat) astride a somber chestnut steed, and a tumbrel full of doomed aristocrats parked next to a guillotine. I flipped the cover open, and scanned the thumbnail description of the plot— the beautiful schoolmistress' daughter, caught by unkind circumstance between the worlds of education and aristocracy and the hired help, forced by fate to make do while a "dark and cruelly handsome" French count thought she was "just the kind of mistress he had to have."

A bright yellow sticker advertised a handwritten price of a dollar. I couldn't resist. I didn't counter, haggle, barter or quibble. This book, I had to have. Reading it, I figured, would be like stepping into a time machine.

The title was vaguely familiar, though at that exact moment I couldn't remember if I'd actually read it before. But since I'd read everything I could get my hands on by Victoria Holt decades earlier, I'd have bet good money I most certainly had.

I'll be the first to confess that as a child, I didn't play well with others. There could be a thousand explanations for that, but we'll skip them all here. Suffice it to say that I read my way through my childhood. Growing up on the northwest side of Chicago, I practically wore grooves in the pavement to the local library at Pulaski and North Avenues, especially in the summertime. No sooner would I finish an armful of books—Greek mythology, Nancy Drew novels, everything the library had about horses, especially the entire Black Stallion series by Walter Farley—then off I trekked, past Woolworth and the Tiffin movie theater and the bowling alley and the delicatessen that carried those boxes of delicious Dutch chocolates but always smelled like smoked herring—arms aching from the load, to return them and bring back another. The window of my second story bedroom fronted on the street, and from the middle of my bed there in the dappled afternoon light I retreated into a world of language and imagery, Homeric adventures and western canyons, mustangs and mysteries.

It didn't do much for my social life ... but it gave me one hell of a great vocabulary and—years later—fabulous verbal scores on my SAT and ACT exams.

Somewhere along the line, though, I outgrew my hunger for stories about teenaged sleuths and Smokey the Cow Pony and turned avidly to a new genre, romantic suspense. Phyllis Whitney, Victoria Holt and

Mary Stewart were my new must-read authors, and my imagination was steeped in tales of young and lovely heroines in difficult circumstances drawn to brooding, distant men who magically turned out alright at the end. Given that my first two years of high school were spent in a sea of plaid jumpers at an all-girls Catholic high school, sightings of actual males of the species were somewhat sporadic, and these books provided a more sophisticated window into love, courtship, and happy endings.

Or so I thought.

Fast forward a few decades, post-divorce, post-motherhood, post-career changes, post-becoming a grownup. Back from the weekend getaway, I wasted little time in finally cracking open a window to a younger, less complicated time. Curled up in bed with a light at my elbow one weekend and a few pillows propped comfortably behind me, doors and windows locked and cat, dog and son soundly asleep, I began to read. But a journey that started with amused anticipation segued quickly into a dutiful slog through repeated disappointment, finishing at long last with a sense of acute nausea ... and relief that it was over.

Good grief, I thought, what mind-warping tripe! What a toxic influence had cast its malignant and formative shadow on such an impressionable young mind!

Knee jerk reaction, of course. Nobody reads romantic suspense to get a dose of reality—all the ormolu clocks and clattering horse-drawn carriages and borrowed evening finery would see to that. But this was ridiculous. I could buy—if pressed—the potential quandary faced by the milquetoast heroine Minella of choosing a loveless if affectionate marriage to the Lord of Derringham Manor, or the reckless and tempestuous life of being the mistress of the sneering, bad-mannered and still-married Comte Fontaine Delibes. But for heaven's sake, did this woman never think outside the childish fantasies of her own mind? Did it never occur to her to just ask someone a question point blank about their motives or their feelings? If someone threw a stone through the window of the chateau, wrapped in a menacing note ... ***do you think that maybe she'd just go tell somebody??***

Patience worn thin, I closed the cover and thought about what to do with this new revelation. The trash can seemed too ... undignified, disrespectful of the past and the arduous journey to the present. Keeping it seemed ... unthinkable. Giving it away to charity ... well, that would be like donating poison to a food bank.

The book sat for weeks in a corner of the living room, as I left daily for work or other errands, paid the bills, toted the firewood, got the oil changed in my car. And then the skies parted, and the ending to this tale became clear.

As evening fell after a day of working in the yard with Chuck and our chain-saws, I stood at the edge of the bonfire blazing with the dusty and cobweb covered scrap lumber I'd pulled from the garage and the mountains of brush we'd cut and dragged from the edge of the driveway and raked into the crackling pile. The heat was a palpable, ominous force, smacking my face and my shins if I stepped just a little too close, but step forward I did anyway from time to time, to drag the smoking vines and branches from the edges back to the middle where they popped and hissed before dissolving into ash. I felt exhausted, but triumphant as well—a primitive goddess of fire-tending.

I'd grown proud of my incremental post-divorce independence over the past couple of years, and I stood surrounded by the fruits of my hitherto most unlikely labors—the tons of gravel moved, the paddock fences repaired, the mulch spread, the plants dug in, the branches trimmed, the shrubs taken down to the ground with a hand saw. And I stood in the shadow of the house where I'd ... fixed the leaky toilet, patched and sanded and painted the bedroom, installed knobs and handles on the basement cabinets, and even managed, after six months of peering through murky darkness on the stairs, to tackle the dreaded light fixture over the foyer.

I pitched the offending book into the fire. And as the sparks wafted upwards in the dark and the flames curled greedily around the pages, I sent the "devil" back home.

Girls in the Graveyard

I was basking like a lizard in the warm Phoenix sun.

Charlie, the nuttier, more persistent half of the canine duo keeping me company on the patio around the turquoise backyard pool hovered, quivering with excitement. He was a big, anxious golden retriever, achingly poised between conflicting imperatives—hang on to his prize, the drool-covered tennis ball gripped tightly in his jaws, or let go of it long enough for me to pick it up and throw it across the yard yet again. The conflict within him played out for anyone to see, as he whipsawed back and forth in front of me, incapable of just choosing a course of action and sticking with it. Bear, an enormous Australian shepherd, hung back and watched with a wolfish stare on his black and silver face.

Two thousand miles away in Wisconsin, a legion of television weather forecasters were beating the steady drum of dire blizzard warnings, unsafe road conditions, imminent airport closings and general natural mayhem. I took another swig of my diet green iced tea and adjusted my spaghetti straps to get the most southern exposure for the effort. I tossed the ball again for Charlie and shut my eyes. A woodpecker rapped persistently at a telephone pole nearby, and a mockingbird called from the edge of the yard. It was good to be here again, and I felt my back muscles start to melt into the mesh seat.

"Here" was my friend Annie B's house in Arizona, and it was her patio furniture I was nestled into so comfortably. I felt sunlight and warmth radiate off the white stucco walls behind and around me. It was my second visit in not very long. The first had come barely a year earlier, when I invited myself down to escape the serious hoopla at my office that would invariably accompany my being there for my birthday—black "over the hill" balloons, silver streamers, and a stuffed buzzard mounted to the back of my chair. The girls in the front of the office take pride in their work. I'd seen it happen, I knew it was coming, the only way to beat the game was to leave town. I hadn't seen Annie B in fifteen years, but she and her husband Vance welcomed me with open arms and started the margaritas flowing as soon as I got there. For the record, I successfully dodged the stuffed buzzard.

Now I was back, along with another friend, Cathy, who'd flown in at the same time from the Twin Cities for some "girlfriend time." The three of us carbon-date back to our first year in college together three decades before. Same dorm, same floor of the same dorm, just a few doors apart, some of the same rambunctious and/or embarrassing memories still woven tightly like threads in the varied tapestries of our lives. We've all assembled good lives, with homes and loved ones and good jobs and great pets and wonderful friends and a sense of purpose and integrity.

But while the ability to connect with people and forge lasting connections and friendships all along the way is the stuff that makes like worth living and keeps our little hearts happily beating … sometimes there's just something really special about getting together with friends who have known you long enough to know where the bones are buried. And who were there, in fact, when you buried them.

I'm not talking anything with a felony status. But lord, it is good to have history!

As befitting the dignity of a graveyard, the bones will remain undisturbed here. Not that there was much dignity associated with some of those bones in the first place. Discretion and circumspection and prudence are not typically the hallmarks of first year college students, and we were no exception to the rule. Students of history will recall that the drinking age was eighteen back then, and every university function came with its own free-flowing keg. Or two. And plastic cups by the hundreds.

As our lives went on, our "bones" involved more adult-style lapses and heartaches: failed romances and failed marriages, missed opportunities and questionable judgments and at least one miscarriage, uncertainties and tears, confessions and agonizing choices. And always, the knowledge that no matter how we reinvented ourselves personally or professionally, no matter how much we morphed deliberately or by chance into the confident, competent women light years removed from those fresh-faced young girls ... years later we could instantly touch that flickering spirit of optimism and newness again simply with the words "do you remember when ...?"

I'm back now from Phoenix, though there are plenty of reminders. A bar of lavender soap bought at the farmer's market bringing me right back there into the desert sunlight and fresh air when I step into the shower. A pair of earrings shaped like coyotes baying at the full moon. Some lemons from the tree in Annie B's front yard, sliced into my tea in the morning. They bring back memories of lovely dinners, and frozen maragaritas made with oranges picked from the trees in the back yard, of conversation and coffee and disclosure and brutal honesty and laughter and a fabulous Rembrandt art exhibit that took our breath away.

But they also remind me of even deeper things, and richer connections, and forgiveness and acceptance and a sense of celebration and bearing witness. And that extraordinary gift only truly comes when ... you know where the bones are buried.

Cordless and Dangerous

The paddock fence was going to have to be fixed, and fixed that day. It was eleven months after the divorce, in which I got the house, the animals, the big sky, and the upkeep on fifteen bucolic acres of Wisconsin countryside. Eleven months after he took all the power tools and the manly knowledge of how to use them.

Now there was a broken board in the wooden fence leaving a space big enough for Babe, my geriatric mare, to sneak through and eat herself to death or disaster in a pasture full of lush green grass. She just couldn't handle eating around the clock at her age. And the duct tape I'd patched things together with just the week before had proved an impermanent solution. The entire board had finally ripped loose from the end post, screws broken off, wood split, little grey shreds of duct tape hanging consumptively from the soft, splintered pine on the ground.

There was an urgency, real and immediate, to the job. I knew in my gut that if I didn't do this thing very soon, my horse would end up dead. I had been taking care of her for most of her life, and she was my last connection to becoming a horse owner at the age of 16. She was also the Calamity Jane of horses when it came to health. She dodged more bullets over the years than I could even begin to remember, though one night spent with her in a barn a few years ago at eight degrees above zero when even the vet thought she would be dead by morning was the high-water mark. I could have bought a really good car—a Jaguar, or a Mercedes—for what I've spent on her over the past three decades.

My options to get someone else to fix the fence were none. After eleven months of "audition" coffees and casual dating, I still wasn't seeing anyone seriously enough to ask him to start pounding nails. And while my ex could still be finagled into the occasional household favor, he was currently floating hundreds of miles away on a houseboat with my children somewhere around International Falls, Minnesota. No, I was truly "home alone." I slipped into a yellow rain jacket, found the retractable measuring tape that sat in a kitchen drawer with my potholders, and went out in the last of the drizzle to gather the exact dimensions of the board and the screws my ex used to build the fence twenty years ago.

I drove to the local Menards and went straight for the power tools. All I knew was that I wanted something cordless. More convenient and less likely to electrocute me if the rain picked up again. My first helper was a polite young man about as old as my third child.

My whole story rushed out at once, of course, as it usually does when I'm treading water in unfamiliar seas. Divorced, on my own, ex-husband with the tools out of town, need to fix something now, totally clueless. He's probably used to it. Sees a middle-aged woman in the power tools aisle looking like a displaced refugee, and thinks, "dear God, why me?" We eventually settled on the store brand package of a cordless drill with a 14.4 volt rechargeable battery and a bunch of drill bits and other parts I didn't recognize. Did he think I'd need a cordless screwdriver too? Not really, he explained, you could do the same thing with the cordless drill. Oh. Well, then.

He stayed on to help me figure out what kind of screws matched up with the old ones. And to find the baling twine. Earlier in the morning, I'd picked my dog up from the kennel, and caught up with Pat, the owner and a friend of mine. She was single too, and a former horse owner, and she got a big laugh at my duct tape improvisation. "Don't forget to buy baling twine," she said as I was leaving. "You'd be amazed at what you can fix with baling twine!"

My cordless drill, a package of screws and a spool of twine in my cart, I headed for the store's lumber yard. Same story spilled out, this time to an itty bitty young girl about half my size with a blonde pony tail. She was delightful. Chatty, friendly, outgoing, helpful to the extreme. She took me under her tiny wing and I followed her through the lumber yard like a puppy.

She not only located the exact size board I needed, but carefully checked over each board to find me a really straight one. Carried it around for me until we got to the checkout lane. In between, she opened up the drill's black plastic carrying case and gave me a tutorial on what I needed to know about using my new tool. She loaded and unloaded the bits, changed the rotation, cautioned me on being safe while using it. She'd followed her dad around a lot when she was little, working alongside him on projects and learning the ins and outs of power tools, saws, many manly and mysterious things. She felt pretty good about it. I felt like a hothouse plant by comparison, but somehow managed to drop into the conversation that I'd gotten a Remington twenty gauge shotgun for Christmas. Female bonding, anyone?

I brought home all the stuff, opened the instruction manual, and knew was in trouble. For all my professional strides over the years—newspaper reporter, freelance writer, prosecutor arguing to the state Supreme Court—our marriage had followed very traditional lines. I baked the cookies and ran the kids and hung the wallpaper, he built the deck and hammered the drywall and set the concrete driveway. Once in a while I'd bring him a glass of cold lemonade while he was working if it was hot out. A building project, to me, was a two-layer cake. My tools were nine-inch round baking pans and a hand mixer. My "secret weapon" in most household emergencies was nail polish remover.

I phoned Tom, my go-to guy with all my manly questions—car maintenance, satellite dishes, tools, you name it. We'd met months ago on line, but weren't dating. He drove a cement truck, and was smart, and funny, and tall, and cute, and sported a diamond earring. I still laugh out loud remembering his e-mails. He, in the middle of watching a NASCAR race on television, was the soul of patience and gave me basic instructions on drilling holes. He cautioned me about not setting the drill to use too much "torque." Huh? I didn't know what he meant, but he assured me that I could break a wrist if I got it wrong. I found the "torque" setting on the drill, figured something in the middle range should keep me out of trouble, and stepped up to the plate.

I had a couple of screw drivers and a scissors in my pocket, my hand saw under one arm, the baling twine under the other, the cordless drill set with a screwdriver head and carried like a six-shooter, and a bunch of two-inch rust-proof deck screws in my pocket. I needed to make a separate trip back for the eight foot board, and as I carried it around, I'd have fit right in with the Three Stooges. Many things got bumped into along the way. I took a moment to mentally praise the sheer brilliance of my ex, who apparently knew that he could buy eight foot boards already cut, set his posts eight feet apart, and avoid all sorts of custom adjustments.

I tried to take the old screws out of the post. The drill battery ran out of juice after the first three. Back to the house I ran for the spare. I used the baling twine to rig a simple scaffold to hold the new board in place, hanging it from the board above, while I position it incrementally to the right spot. Yes, my friend Pat was right—you CAN use baling twine for almost anything!!

The board exactly in place, I took one of the new screws from my pocket, and tried to drill the screw into the board. It didn't make a dent. Back to the house again, I switched from the screwdriver head to a drill bit. Tired of the round trips, I tested the drill bit out on a piece of firewood in the living room. Sawdust flew, but it worked.

Finally fully equipped, I set to the task at hand. The drill bit peeled right through the board and into the post below, leaving tiny spits of wood in its wake. I could feel the difference in pressure as it ripped first through the new plank of wood, and then grabbed deeper into the softer, old post beneath. I remember the only thing I understood from the instruction manual, and kept the drill bit turning as I pulled it out of the board. By golly, I'd made a real, live, professional-looking HOLE!!! I twisted a screw in with a hand-held screwdriver, and breathed a sigh of satisfaction when it held the board fast. The rest of the job went quickly. So quickly, in fact, that I decided to inspect the rest of the fence. I found that another board has completely broken in half as well, but had escaped notice, hidden by some low hanging pine branches.

Well. No kids around, no bugs flying around either because of the heavy rains, nobody to interfere with another job, hey, I was on a roll.

I drove back to Menards, sauntered in the lumber yard entrance, and found the same young girl. We located yet another fabulously straight eight foot board for this second project, and she seemed genuinely happy and excited for me that I was starting to have fun with this. I told her about the baling twine scaffold, and she seemed truly impressed. "That's really smart," she says. "I would have probably just wrestled with it myself." I felt like I'd been given the Order of the British Empire.

Returning to the paddock, I set to work with a hand saw, getting rid of the overhanging pine branches so that I could reach the broken board. There were more branches to trim than I thought, and more work all around than I could have imagined. The lush, green boughs were each about ten feet long, and heavy as I dragged them away to a corner of the pasture. I was sweating, and getting covered with sap and lichen and sawdust. The mare watched from a distance, her gold coat and white mane gleaming prettily in the afternoon sun as she munched her way through a field of grass and Queen Anne's Lace.

Nothing went smoothly. One of the old screws broke off in the post, leaving the twisted, spiral stem jutting like a brash taunt to my inexperience. I took the business end of the hammer and bashed the broken screw into the post until the surface was once again flat. Out of sight, out of mind. I somehow felt a whole lot better for pounding something hard.

This time, the board was an inch too long. Or the space it was supposed to fit in was an inch too short. It could be that the old posts had shifted over twenty years, or that the other boards swelled from the earlier rain. I lugged the board down to the second basement that doubled as my ex's workshop. Nothing useful in sight except for a small vise. Clamping one end of the board in place, balancing the other on a cardboard box, I turned again to my little hand saw and hoped to heaven that I could cut in a straight line. This was WAY different than lopping off odd branches, this required actual precision. I guessed at what an inch would be, and tentatively scraped the teeth across the top of the board. Sawdust scattered every which way, and the saw skittered across the top, directionless, the teeth never taking hold. I tried again. The same thing happened.

I remembered that failure was not an option. This time I grabbed the saw handle with both hands, and drew the teeth across the board like I was the one in charge. Amazingly, a notch formed and the blade dropped in a straight line through the pine. An inch-wide strip of wood fell to the floor, leaving an edge that looked straight, and consistent, and premeditated.

One more trip back to the paddock with the shortened board, and the job finally went the way I'd planned … an hour earlier. Baling twine, drill bit, Phillips screwdriver, all feeling familiar, in a final get-it-done-and-get-out rhythm. Board firmly in place, I gathered up the drill, the screwdrivers, the screws, the twine, the scissors, the saw, and dragged them back to the house. As I brought the mare in from the pasture, happy knowing that there was no way she'd getting loose that night, I realized I'd forgotten to cut down the loops of baling twine. It broke up the horizontal lines of the newly fixed fence like an odd little bit of macramé. After a second's thought, I decided to leave them there. If they ever come loose, birds can use the strands for nesting material. But for now, every time I see them, I smile.

The Tale of the Christmas Axes

Martha Stewart, stop reading right now. I can't be held responsible for the stroke sure to follow if you find out about last Christmas at my house. It's all about what happens when you finally turn over the reins of control. In the end, you laugh a lot harder.

My friend Barb and I could be templates for that tired stereotype, "women who do too much." Not because we're perfect, but because we're both coming from behind. Barb's still got some recuperation issues from back and neck surgery that slow her down from time to time. And after a riding accident eleven years ago, I still run out of steam—and the ability to just keep standing—on a long day earlier than I used to. Which doesn't keep either of us from pulling out all the stops at the holidays.

Three of the four kids were coming home from college or beyond right before Christmas, and I wanted the short time they could all spend together to be as cozy as a Norman Rockwell picture turned into a Hallmark television movie. There was a wreath on the door, and a nine foot Christmas tree with dozens of glass-blown and hand-embroidered ornaments, strung with strings of red wooden "cranberries," festooned with ceramic birds and various cute critters. Homemade pumpkin pie, homemade banana muffins, homemade Christmas cookies in four varieties. Needlepoint stockings hung by the chimney with care.

So what if I couldn't find the crèche for the second year running, I found the stuffed moose that sings "Grandma Got Run Over By a Reindeer" and put fresh batteries in it before they got home. Somebody sat on it as if on cue, and the moose started to sing. Sixty pounds of fresh firewood in the wrought iron stand next to the fireplace, along with a basket of "fatwood" to start the fire in a hurry. Coffee in the pot, and whipped cream to go on the hot chocolate.

But the high point for fun has always been rolling out and decorating the butter cookies. And this time was no exception. They set to the task almost as soon as Michael, the freshman, walked in the door and dumped his gear. By this time it was late afternoon, and I was done in after days of shopping and wrapping and baking. And two days spent on a last-minute felony drug trial. I poured myself a glass of wine, pulled down the bowl of cookie cutters from the top shelf, and handed off the rolling pin to the younger generation. "Knock yourselves out," I said, and sat down on the sofa to read the paper as the flames danced in the hearth.

The kitchen was like a beehive, and I enjoyed the energy from a distance. As soon as the last batch of cookies was finished and cooling, we had dinner and ripped into the present exchange. Then the kids left to go open presents at their dad's house, and I finally started to take inventory of what they'd left behind.

It looked like a holiday bomb had gone off. Every open surface was covered with flour, or gingerbread crumbs, or frosting. Red sugar crystals. Green sugar crystals. Candy hearts, candy sprinkles, candy flowers. Discarded coffee cups and wine glasses were everywhere. Cookies were everywhere, too, and as I started to pick them up to store them, I laughed out loud.

My late mother in law had given me the cookie cutters two decades ago, and every year I'd pulled out the most obvious holiday ones: there was Santa, and an angel, a reindeer, a fir tree, a bell, a star, a heart, a flower. And every year, for some reason, the censor in me had passed on pulling out the cutter clearly shaped like an axe. Why Santa might need an axe on his journeys, I can only guess. But the kids found the axe-shaped cookie cutter in the bottom of the bowl I'd handed them, and had taken it to town.

There were lots and lots of Christmas axes in this cookie collection. Bloody axes, in fact, as they'd decorated the edges of the blades with red sugar crystals. Keeping the theme going, they'd brought the angels into the act as well, with bloody little angel hands to go with the little bloody axes. I was surprised they left Santa with his head on his shoulders. The extra dreadlocks they added to Rudolph's antlers and colored red, making him the "Sideshow Bob" of the reindeer team, seemed almost like an afterthought. I packed cookies and laughed. Then I packed some more cookies, and laughed some more.

The next day I called Barb to tell her about our new Christmas tradition. She had one of her own to match. Seems she ran out of holiday steam a bit early too, and turned the task of decorating the gingerbread men at her house over to a twelve year old niece. From now on, gingerbread men at her house will now have three eyes instead of the standard two.

It's always nice to have tradition to look forward to. Next time, if the kids want to do bloody Christmas axes and murderous angels again, I'll make sure they've got red frosting to do the job right.

End of the taxi line

Twenty five years of being "Mom's Taxi" ended with a spritz of suntan lotion and a wave, a backward glance and a promise to be home by six thirty for supper. Then I watched the Ford Escape pull off down the driveway, my sixteen year old son at the wheel, his driver's license only two hours old, nary a scratch or a smudge on it.

An afternoon at a friend's swimming pool beckoned on this ninety degree day as a fine reward for getting a perfect score on his road test. To his credit—and mine—he stuck around long enough for me to get home from running errands to make sure he was basted in enough sunblock to keep from frying as he floated and gloated.

The metaphorical silence was eerie as I walked into the house and absorbed the fact that I could pick whatever task I wanted to do without calculating when I would have to interrupt it and make a taxi run.

I use the word "silence" loosely, since it's never quiet in the country. The cicadas haven't even arrived yet, but there are trucks rattling past on the nearby highway and the occasional emergency siren, crickets, dogs barking, owls hooting, goldfinches jostling for perch space and loudly doing the dozens on the thistle feeder below the living room window, an infinitesimally small warbler making outrageously loud chatters and chirps and streams of melody, warning others to stay away from that dead snag where she's nesting. But there was a strange silence in my heart anyway.

A quarter century of my life has been spent behind the wheel of my car—first a sedan, then a station wagon, upgraded to a mini-van, and finally an SUV—driving my children to their destinations. From the first newborn, off to a well-baby checkup, anxiously awaiting a pediatrician's imprimatur that indeed all was well and developmentally on track, to the sixteen year old delivered to the last morning final exam I would ever have to detour to the high school on the way to work, I have manned the wheel.

In mileage, I've circled the globe several times over. Girl Scout outings, summer camp, Little League, soccer tournaments, tennis meets, pole-vaulting competitions, school supply runs. Trips to the doctor, trips to the emergency room, trips to the bus stop, trips to the mall. The march of progress has been measured not only by the number of strategically concealed grey hairs on my head but by the tread on my tires and the price of gas.

I may have forgotten most of the details … though not the fact that some unnamed child once left a bag of potato chips in the mesh magazine rack behind the driver's seat in my first Subaru and a mouse chewed a hole in the fabric to get to the goodies … but not the good feelings. Like many a taxi driver, I liked to keep the conversation rolling. And as sons and daughters got older and busier, it was during those five and ten minute stretches between pickups and drop-offs that connections stayed alive, politics got argued, venting got spilled, unfairness of every ilk was examined. On longer trips of several hours, silence often reigned as a teenager running on empty set the passenger seat back and settled in for much-needed nap, a fleece blanket wrapped around tired shoulders. I felt as much a flood of tenderness then as I did when I tucked them in to bed at night as babies.

I don't do transitions well. Just ask the kids how I reacted to the idea of moving the living room furniture a few years ago.

Stepping out of the car at the high school that morning, Robert casually reminded me "Hey Ma, this is the last day you'll have to do this!" Then the door shut and I was alone with my reverie and my sense of shock. I had been so focused on getting to work, my mind racing ahead to just how many minutes late I'd be arriving at the office,

I hadn't even marked the day. I pouted, deflated and sorrowed, for the rest of the ride.

Yes, I know I'm in the minority. Most mothers I know have done a jig when their youngest children finally got their driver's licenses. And yes, the closing of one chapter always means the beginning of another. I'm already looking ahead to new adventures—more travel, more time to write, more time to sit and think. I'm making new discoveries already—some in my garden, some from the back of a Harley.

But I won't be retiring my "Mom's Taxi" coffee mug from the kitchen cabinet any time soon. The memories it holds are too sweet.

The Island

The feeling never gets old. As the ferry boat's engines roar to life and the boat pulls away from the dock, the weight of reality slips from your shoulders like a silk scarf caught by the breeze and carried away, to vanish like a magician's sleight of hand. Looking forward, from the vehicle deck closer to the water, the cold spray of dark waves cut by the ferry's prow is bracing, awakening. Looking backward, the endless woods surrounding the dock and leaning over the shoreline gradually diminish to nothing as the ferry gamely shoulders it way across Death's Door to Washington Island.

The journey was one of many I'd taken over the years, but the first one I was making alone.

The first had been nearly twenty years before. My friend Liz had a family vacation cabin on the island, and invited me to bring my two young daughters to visit for a few days one summer. Her husband was in medical school, and she often took her own girls up there for extended stays, to the island where she had spent her summers growing up.

The trip was an odyssey in every sense. Sensible minivan filled with two car seats, girls aged two and four, a chocolate chip cheesecake with a chocolate crumb crust, a four-pack of wine coolers, and other toys, accessories and accoutrements and beach toys for several days. We drove an unfamiliar route for hours, through the entirety of the enormous peninsula jutting like a thumb into Lake Michigan, all the way to land's end and the ferry dock where we waited for the next stage of the adventure.

Fares paid, we followed like sheep as the line of cars and trucks was guided one by one by the crew into four parallel lines on the boat, nearly bumper to bumper. Then, ignition turned off, we climbed the narrow metal stairs and settled in on a bench on the passenger deck. I clutched the girls in a death grip, afraid that they might lean too far over the side rail.

A half hour later, with windblown hair, sunburned cheeks and a sense of wonder, we disembarked and started following more directions to the cabin. We drove several miles as far north as we could, then turned east and drove clear to the far side of the island. Another turn north, and we eventually found ourselves driving to the outermost edge of the island, down a gravel path through pines and hardwoods.

The cabin sat in a clearing, with white siding and a red roof gleaming prettily in the sun. Beyond the house was a bluff, and at the edge of the bluff, fifty foot birch trees swayed, their leaves glinting in the sun, as the Lake Michigan waves glittered in the distance like diamond dust. The air was clear and pure, and I felt like I'd arrived at the gates of heaven.

For years after that maiden voyage, we returned to the island as a family for a week every summer, with two children, then three, then four. The days were lazy, spent mostly at the beach, with occasional forays to the gift shops for souvenirs and ice cream. Eventually, though, the kids outgrew the sense of wonder at finding yet another clam shell in the water, and we found other places to vacation. Once the inevitable dissonance of college scheduling clashed with the local school year for the younger ones, it became hard to schedule family vacations at all.

But here I was, heading back to the island again, wondering whether I'd had a good idea.

The island wasn't my first choice. The summer before, I had spent a week at a writer's retreat on the peninsula. It was nurturing, encouraging, inspiring, invigorating, thought-provoking, and came with all meals included and prepared. I had planned to return for the replenishment of my writer's soul, but could not get the week off work.

So I dried my tears, and resolutely booked a tiny affordable cabin on the island, on the water, for a week when I could get away, when the boys would be out West in a camping adventure with their Dad.

I brought a laptop, my notebooks, a week's worth of Lean Cuisine meals and a carton of Instant Breakfast packets. Heading north on the interstate, condensation dripping on the mocha frappuccino in the cup holder next to me, I had fleeting pangs of uncertainty about whether I could handle the solitude; the memories; the passage of time; the reminders of broken dreams. I needn't have worried.

The cabin was tiny, and prosaic, with a yard and deck mostly surrounded by cedars but with a clear line of sight from the back door across the deck, through the yard and to the shore beyond. If I parked myself just right on a lounge chair, a diet soda next to me and my binoculars nearby, I could sit for hours and not leave the spot.

I wrote. I journaled. I read for the fun of it. I napped when I felt like it. I walked three miles every morning on quiet country roads that felt like cathedral naves. I bird-watched with a vengeance. I drove into town every day to pick up a copy of the Chicago Tribune, an ice cream bar and a candy bar, retreating back to my fortress of solitude to read the paper on the deck. I started the vacation by reading a few chapters of Henry David Thoreau's "Walden" on the first evening, putting me in an excellent frame of mind for appreciating nature. I re-read "Gift from the Sea" by Anne Morrow Lindbergh from cover to cover.

From the deck I watched a bald eagle soar around a nearby bird refuge, and a broad-winged hawk depart my yard with a snake clutched in his talons. I watched a pair of mute swans and their two little cygnets swim around the refuge nearly every day. In an interesting balancing of priorities, I weighed whether to check out the open trap-shoot or attend a poetry reading/discussion group about Emily Dickenson, unfortunately scheduled for the same evening. Civility won out, though I felt a bit like a Neanderthal crashing an Edwardian dinner party. Had a terrific time nonetheless.

Despite the low lake level, I finally found a shallow, crystalline, sand-bottomed bay in a nature preserve, and visited often, stretched out in the water while little quicksilver fish swam around me in curiosity. I watched an osprey return to land from hunting on the lake, his dinner suspended beneath him. I saw damselflies so brilliantly turquoise that I thought the first one was a piece of cast-off plastic, and dodged dragonflies the size of B-52s. One evening, a little tired of the flat, placid shoreline at my cabin, I went searching for crashing waves.

I found them off Carlin's Point. It took a half-mile hike in from the road to the nature preserve, then another quarter mile out across rocky, weedy flats where the lake shore used to be. Then further across slimy, rocky weedy flats, and then across slippery rocky shallows, until the water grew deeper and I finally had waves crashing on my knees. The wind nearly pushed me over, but it felt glorious. I stared in amazement at the aerial skill of a seagull hovering above my right shoulder, brilliant white against the blue sky, suspended in this gale seemingly effortlessly. I watched a great blue heron fishing out on a rocky islet, and felt an instant sisterly bond with a red-breasted merganser hen and her thirteen little ducklings who hung around my shoreline. Through all the years I'd been a soccer mom, I'd always said I'd felt like a mother duck.

The week passed quickly. I'd spent basically every minute of good weather outdoors, face down on the lounge chair on the deck or face down on a blanket in a dune at the shore. There was only the sound of the waves in the distance and the wind up close, sunlight dappling through birch trees and cedars, birds singing nearby, and the feeling of being hooked up to some giant life support system that was pumping something vital back into me.

The end of a trip to the island always comes, not when you return home, but when your car tires finally grab pavement on the mainland off the ferry. This time was no different. But as I meandered my way home, on no particular timetable, so relaxed I was still nearly boneless, I thought …

Yes, the island was a good idea.

Wildflower seeds and beer

It started with a handful of small red and white carnations in a glass Coke bottle, propped charmingly and invitingly in the cup holder of a fifteen year old navy blue Ford pickup truck. It was February, and the dead of winter, and the slush at the curb was up to my ankles when I stepped out to the pavement on the way to an evening of Irish dancing. Flower gardening, never a successful hobby, was the furthest thing on my mind. Staying warm and dry was more like it.

A proper bouquet followed a few days later, and then the next week, a gift of a miniature rosebush with perfect white blooms and sturdy green foliage. It sat on the kitchen counter until the blooms shriveled, and the leaves dropped, and I finally put it out on the back porch to get some actual sunlight and toughen up. If it was going to live here, it was going to have to fend for itself.

When it comes to gardening, I freely admit to having a "black thumb." Not black as in fecund, fertile, life-giving soil, Earth Mother, goddess of fertility and all things abundant. Black like the kiss of death. My ability to kill indestructible plants is legendary. Philodendrons. Cactuses. Even Venus Fly Traps ... and for heaven's sake, those things are like wild animals, they catch their own prey and feed themselves.

But the man who has laid siege to my heart for the past several months with a tidal wave of thoughtfulness, likes to garden. No, that doesn't do it justice. He's full-tilt nuts about it. Happy, happy, happy when he's digging in some more English daisies or a new variety of columbine. Lots of things in his yard are watered regularly, and mulched, and tended, and flourishing. And it is forever a work in progress. "Done" is not a word in his vocabulary.

The stretch of ground around my house, on the other hand, looked like Death Valley. I'd had stone facing attached to the lower level of the house last fall, and all that remained of the few straggly rose bushes that used to snatch at my ankles around August, begging for water, and three huge bushes that had to come down for the workmen to maneuver were a handful of ugly stumps and some peony shoots. We sat on his back porch one warm spring day, surveying his flower beds, and he explained that he was really, really getting the urge to garden for about the next month. And it was going to either be his garden or mine. "How about mine?" I said. And so the fuse was lit.

My soul began to stir, but in small increments at first. I went out to a couple of garden stores and bought rose bushes. A couple of big expensive ones, in a spirit of cautious optimism, but mostly bushes that ran no more than five bucks. If I was going to kill them, if they were really dead plants walking, I didn't want to spend a lot. I bought a new set of gardening gloves for three ninety-nine. They were sky blue with little pink tulips on the backs. I felt as ready as I'd ever be.

He showed up the next Sunday with the truck loaded with gardening tools, a boom box, a bunch of rock and roll CDs, his teenage daughter, a chain saw and some beer. I weeded and yanked out rotted gardening cloth from beneath mouldering wood chips, served lunch and pondered where to put the new roses. He chain sawed the stumps to practically nothing, dug out and reset the timbers framing the rose beds to ground level, raked stones out of the dirt and dug the holes for the rose bushes. When the first of the two rose beds were done, we took a break and stood off to the side, admiring the promise of the half dozen leafless plants we had planted and drenched with water. The dirt was flat and bare, just waiting demurely for a coverlet to look decent.

"So where does a girl go for mulch?" I asked. Was I supposed to buy it at the garden store by the bag? Order it from a landscape supply place in bulk? Get it delivered by the bushel?

"Oh, I've got that in the back of the truck," he said. Zing went the strings of my heart, and I felt my knees go weak. When he left, hours later, my universe had been transformed. Stepping out of my front door, I could see a straight line of rose bushes to the left and right, neatly edged, weed-free, prettily mulched with shredded cedar. "Oh man, this is like a canvas just waiting to come to life!" he said proudly before he drove off. His enthusiasm was a catchy as a wildfire in a drought.

The next project was far more ambitious. A two hundred square foot area next to the house covered by about two and a half tons of gravel with plastic sheeting underneath. I had looked at it like Sisyphus must have looked up that mountain after the first few fruitless tries at pushing that boulder uphill. I knew that with a veritable crew of gardeners and a baron's budget, something could be accomplished, but this was too big a job for one or two people. My muse was not dissuaded. "Man, you could really put a garden in here!" he grinned and started planning.

The next Sunday, we would rendezvous with shovels and his rototiller and start digging, and see how far we got. Hope began to stir in my heart a little more, one tiny corner at a time. I began to look through expensive gardening catalogs for things I thought were pretty, then made nearly daily trips to the upscale garden store about a mile from my house looking for them priced cheaper in four inch pots.

He brought me a goldfinch feeder and ten pounds of thistle seed to fill it with. I bought a double shepherd's hook to hang it from, and a hanging basket of geraniums to balance it out. He brought me a watering wand. I hooked a hose up to the spigot by the front door. I bought a few pansies and geraniums to put in pots around the front of the house, then went searching for some lightweight and artistic pots to put them in. I bought dirt. I bought nemesia, which I'd never heard of before, but it's an annual that looks like a mass of tiny orchids, so cute that I had to have it, even if I'd have to think of where to put it later. I bought lavender, and coneflowers, and coreopsis, and three kinds of delphiniums, and coral bells, and evening primroses, and daylilies and phlox. I even bought a butterfly bush. Then six.

I picked my son up from school one day, bursting with accomplishment at nabbing three tall matching deep blue delphiniums with white centers at the local garden store, alleged to eventually reach heights of up to six feet. They'd make a nice counterpoint to the white butterfly bush nearby. I was SO PROUD! My son looked at me with his eyes glazing over. Remember the the teacher those old "Charlie Brown" cartoons? "Wah, wah wah, wah wah …" Or the "blah, blah, blah …" that Bart Simpson hears when Mrs. Krabapple is talking? Well, that was the look I got. But nothing could rain on my parade!

The gravel-moving project was just as much work as it sounded like, but somehow we got it done over the course of two weekends. Plastic was removed, extra rocks raked out, dirt tilled, plants put in and watered. My son helped us replant phlox and a pair of peonies from a long-abandoned garden attempt while I ran to buy more mulch. And somehow, during that first day of digging and sweating, the unexpected question was broached, "now where would you like a wildflower garden?" Huh what? Yes, a genuine wildflower garden could be mine … if I would only pick out the spot to be roto-tilled, and then make a run to the garden store for some wildflower seeds. Oh, and pick up some beer on the way back. What a shopping list! I drove, he roto-tilled. I found some seeds at the garden center, indulged my fancy for another half dozen perennials, and brought back a six pack of Michelob in icy cold glass bottles.

We're finally close to being done for this year … though "done" in a gardener's vocabulary is a vague concept. Most of the perennial plants are in, I've finished putting annuals in pots, and the wildflowers have started to sprout. I can see them bursting from the soil a little more every day. We bought a half ton of Arizona sandstone, drove it home in the pickup truck, sledgehammered it into smaller pavers, and set it into a pretty, staggered footpath through the garden.

Inspired to action, I even shoveled away some more gravel on the other side of the house, ripped out the plastic, broke up the dirt with a shovel, and put in daylily garden … all by myself! The fever has been catching, along with the joy. For Mother's Day, my younger son bought me some solar powered lanterns to show off the new garden, and a pretty pink mum which I planted proudly at the forefront of things. I'm spending more time watering plants than I could have ever believed, but it's a tranquility zone while I'm doing it. And now that they're being watered once in a while, my rose bushes have never looked so good.

Lest I get too cocky, though, I need look no further than the last part of that Mother's Day gift. My son is thrilled to death with the way the gardens have turned out, and how nice they make the house look when he walks up the drive. Happy, too, to see me smile as radiantly as I have been for the past couple of months since this new familiarity with growing things has taken hold, and the way I've blossomed along with the coreopsis and the phlox.

But the last word, based on my track record to date, sits carved on a decorative rock in the garden, ready to be moved into position as circumstances and fate should dictate. "I Tried, But It Died." I hope I don't have to use it.

At any rate, I still have the Coke bottle.

The Carpe Diem girls

The Mississippi River rolled smoothly beneath us as we leaned on the railing, resting on our elbows, into the light breeze. Live bluegrass music floated forward from a small group of musicians in the enclosed rear section of the cruise boat.

My daughters and I soaked up the tranquility of the warm evening, the last of Indian summer, like contented sponges. We'd grabbed what we thought were the best seats on the boat. Right up front, with no one else standing between us and the river as we slowly cut our swath through sultry, languid side channels and the river main. We laughingly passed a bottle of white wine, bought earlier that day at a winery across the river in Iowa, between us. Paper cups scrounged from our bed and breakfast stood in for fancy stemware. And we acknowledged, though briefly, that we each had our reasons for looking at life a little differently now, as a lot more precious and finite and precarious, as "before and after."

My own moment of reckoning came twelve years ago, though at the exact moment I must say I was too preoccupied with surviving it to look at the deeper ramifications. Only two months after actor Christopher Reeve was paralyzed from the neck down in a horseback riding accident, I took a long fall from a tall horse going over a jump and hit the ground, hard. My back hit first, then my head. I remember lying in the sandy dirt of the riding arena, blue skies and tree boughs above me, wondering when it would stop hurting enough for me to breathe again.

After some dickering and bickering and negotiating—I was sure I'd be "just fine"—an ambulance was called. I was strapped to a board, lifted in like a piece of lumber, and transported to a nearby hospital. I remember swapping horse stories on the ride down with one of the EMTs who used to own some Appaloosas. An exam and some paperwork and a CT scan later, doctors delivered the bad news: I had a broken back. A vertebra halfway down my spine had fractured. No, I wouldn't be going home that night. I was shocked. Serious accidents were something that happened to other people, not me.

In a pain-killer induced haze, I remember some doctor explaining that it was too risky to try to stabilize the break surgically, so the plan would be to let it heal on its own. I was catheterized and confined to bed for five days, while the swelling in my back muscles went down enough that I could finally be wrapped in fiberglass from collarbones to hips and sent home. Three months of aggravation, discomfort and taking no deep breaths (not to mention no showers) ensued, followed by a good year or two of the kind of pain and weakness that even now still lingers.

It was a watershed for me. "Life's short, take chances, trust your instincts," were the themes that rose to the top of the philosophical pile. I'd taken that fence a second time at the confident urging of my riding instructor but against my better judgment and some strong argument. "See, I told you so," seemed a churlish and petty way to view a grave situation, but I emerged with the indelible conviction to give that "inner voice" a much better hearing as well as a final say from now on. And to make the most out of every day I had left.

There was no rhyme or reason to luck, I knew, no sense at all to be made of the fact that after our equestrian accidents, Christopher Reeve was in a wheelchair and on a ventilator, and I was still driving the car pool to gymnastic practice.

And so I found my voice. Looked back at the fork in the road made fifteen years earlier—journalism or law—and gave the road less traveled a try. Got more accustomed to first recognizing, and then saying, "I want this. I **need** this." Went to law school, flourished like a flower in the desert suddenly blessed by a deluge, picked a career in criminal prosecution. And was reminded every day, by the ache in my back, of how fragile we are.

My daughters have also had their own reasons for looking down the maw of mortality and coming away changed, valuing every shining moment. Anna Quindlen described this awakening well in her book "A Short Guide to a Happy Life," when she wrote about her mother's illness and death from ovarian cancer when Quindlen was only a nineteen year old college student. We've each experienced what she called that "dividing line between seeing the world in black and white, and in Technicolor. The lights came on, for the darkest possible reason."

We take little in the way of happiness for granted these days, and so after months of trading busy schedules, we booked a weekend for just the three of us to meet in Prairie du Chien to do a whole lot of nuthin' … and anything else we could come up with. For two and a half days we flew by the seat of our pants. Laughed and picked our way through a flea market in Iowa, ate chili and bison burgers at the Marquette Café, sampled wines at the Eagle's Landing winery, shopped for antiques and candles and knicknacks at too many places to remember. Snacked every once in a while on a bag of Honeycrisp apples we bought at a roadside stand and a Ziploc tub of homemade apple dip I'd brought along for the heck of it. (Made of cream cheese, brown sugar, chopped peanuts and vanilla, it's one of those "perfect foods"—a combination of fat, sugar, and just a big enough fig leaf of protein to justify its existence.) Signed up for the sunset bluegrass cruise down the Mississippi, hiked along the Iowa bluffs along the river.

The cruise was heavenly, the music wonderful, the evening temperature perfect as the sun dropped lower in the sky. As we gazed, and drank, and admired, one of the musicians took a little while to recount spending a few weeks up in the mountains with his son— New Mexico, I think—as they camped in rudimentary conditions and watched hawks together, a shared passion. He spoke warmly, and fondly, and eloquently of time with his son in soaring, splendid surroundings, of beautiful skies and cold nights and meals cooked on a camp stove. I never turned around. Just thought, "oh, that's sweet … now how about another song?" My younger daughter, Sarah, bought one of their CDs at the end of the cruise, and read us the liner notes as we drove around after breakfast.

The next day we crossed over the Mississippi into Iowa again, to Effigy Mounds National Monument, where we hoped to find a hiking trail that wouldn't do us in. The day once again was gorgeous, warm and sunny, with a light breeze. The parking lot was packed, filled with families and other birdwatchers gathered to view the annual hawk migration taking place. We saw a bald eagle flying above as we walked from the parking lot to the visitor center.

A large white tent was set up nearby for T-shirt sales and music CDs. A small sign announced that the proceeds from the T-shirt sale would be going to support the family of somebody or other. The name rankled slightly, and I cast around for a stronger thread of memory. We looked the T-shirts over, started examining the CDs. Sarah stood at my elbow. "Hey, wait a minute," I asked. "Isn't that the same name as those guys on the boat from last night?" She wasn't sure.

I walked to another side of the tent. A newspaper article was on display, a long and moving tribute to a young musician and his three year old son who had died recently in a car accident. It spoke richly of his family, and of his father, also a musician and fellow environmentalist and hawk fancier. And a sad chill spread through me as I thought of the mid-music narrative from the night before, that fond reminiscence by a father about spending irreplaceable time in the mountains with his son. How he could speak at all amidst grief so deep was beyond me. And it reminded me once again of just how quickly life can turn on a dime, and that opportunities to say "I love you" should never be passed over.

We found a trail that took us, panting in the heat, to the top of the bluffs, to a picturesque view where we could look over the glittering river far below that we had skimmed the surface on just the night before. Once we walked back down, we knew, the weekend together would be over. There would be hugs and kisses and waves goodbye through car windows, but we each had a hundred miles or more ahead of us, and a return to the daily grind and responsibilities. We lingered, soaking in the sunlight sparkling through the tree branches, feeling the wind in our hair, and congratulating ourselves for making it this far.

If we had the ability to change the past, I'm sure that each of us would summon a magic wand to undo the things that gave us such an appreciation that time is fleeing, and that life is fragile, and that beauty is everywhere and often found in small things. But of course we can't. All we can do is gratefully wake up every morning, and think ... "carpe diem."

Of Shoes and Strategy

They were "death on a staircase" shoes, and they stopped me dead in my tracks.

Sleek leopard print brocade, with pointy toes, squared off vamps, delicate sling backs, and spike heels that added a good three and a half inches to my height. These were definitely trophy shoes.

I tried them on, but the questions I purported to be seriously asking myself as I strode back and forth in the shoe department glancing at the mirror from various angles—could I *really* wear them into a courtroom; what suit and accessories would they *possibly* go with; if I didn't think I'd wear them to work where on *earth* would I ever wear them—were as ritualized and formulaic as Kabuki theater.

Of course I was going to buy them, it was a foregone conclusion. They were gorgeous, and sexy, and the fact I had no place in particular to wear them yet hadn't been a deterrent to any of their predecessors sitting in my closet and getting regular workouts. My theory that the occasion would follow the shoes was still working just fine, thank you very much. The shoes came home with me.

Spike heels get a bum rap from a lot of quarters. They've been likened to Chinese foot-binding. A male conspiracy to keep us helpless and off balance. Something that channels the pain of the wearer into the suffering and domination of someone else. A recent article in National Geographic Magazine, "Every Shoe Tells a Story," quoted British photographer David Bailey as having a fondness for high heels because "[i]t means girls can't run away from me."

46

If that's what Mr. Bailey really said, I don't think he was grasping the whole picture.

Doesn't anybody remember what Jennifer Jason Leigh's evil character did to Bridget Fonda's boyfriend with a stiletto heel in the 1992 movie "Single White Female"? Or how Rachel McAdams slowed down terrorist bad-guy Cillian Murphy toward the end of director Wes Craven's 2005 thriller "Red Eye"? I had to laugh when I watched the scene where she sinks her sling-back stiletto into Murphy's thigh, realizing, *I have those very same shoes*!! And we've all seen what Jack Bauer is capable of doing with his bare hands week after week in "24." Just imagine what he could do armed with a pair of Manolo Blahniks. Probably break into Fort Knox blindfolded and walking backwards.

I like to break down my own fondness for "limousine shoes" as an exercise in courtroom strategy, since nearly every pair that follows me home in a shopping bag finds it way into court with me at some point.

First, there's the height advantage, always a good thing in an authority figure. At five foot ten in heels, I'm easy to spot in a crowd. Then, of course, there's that delightfully authoritative snap of spike heels on a marble floor, an auditory declaration that indeed, trouble is just around the corner and closing fast. A cop I worked with daily until his retirement said he could tell that I was approaching a particular courtroom from behind closed doors just by the rapping sound of my footsteps in the corridor beyond. I like it that way!

And last—aside from the whole "armed and dangerous" aspect of wearing something that could literally put somebody's eye out—is what I call the "mother-in-law" advantage. Hard to really pinpoint this one, except to feel that on some level, if a defendant's mother, or sister, or aunt suddenly stops our group problem-solving discussion to tell me that I've got great shoes, well, I've gained … something. Not sure what, but … something that none of my male colleagues in wing-tips or oxfords will ever experience a glimpse of.

Which brings me to one of my favorite illustrations of just why I keep wearing these death-defying shoes to court, and taking the elevator instead of risking my life on the stairs. A few months ago, criminal traffic court—the stuff that can get you jail time—was about to start. The defendants' names are usually called in alphabetical order, or in whatever order a judge feels like mixing up the alphabet just to keep things interesting that day.

A middle-aged woman came up to me and asked if I could do her a favor by getting her case called early in the bunch. Her husband had cancer, and was home alone, and she needed to get back to help him with his medications. Was there anything I could do? She was nervous and clearly out of her element here, not one of our more experienced customers who take their repeat appearances in stride, the "not guilty" plea as reflexive as breathing. I remember I was wearing a pair of show-stopping plaid stilettos that day, with tiny black patent bows, and I absolutely towered over her in them. She barely came past my chin.

I assured her that I would do what I could, and passed word to the judge that this woman could really use a favor. He called her case in a hurry, and she was gracious and effusive in her thanks to all for letting her be on her way in such short order under such difficult circumstances. As she was leaving, she passed me as I sat at the prosecution table and smiled on her way out. They she caught herself in mid-stride, turned, and in front of a room full of defendants, attorneys, courtroom staff and the judge, breached decorum, stopped, and announced "oh, and I love your shoes!!"

The prosecution rests.

Ripple Effect

She looked familiar, but somehow shorter. For an embarrassing instant, I couldn't remember her name. But she was grabbing me by both elbows and smiling and anybody could tell she was REALLY happy to see me!

I was standing in the middle of Miss Katie's Diner, a retro-fifties restaurant near Marquette University with a whole lot of steel and chrome, waitresses in bobby sox, and cheeseburgers to die for. I'd just finished lunch during a break from an annual criminal law conference that a few of the guys from work and I go to every December to find out just how much we don't know about our jobs. Our little foursome stood up and shrugged into our coats, heading for the door, looking a lot like a casual, weekend version of the intro to "Law & Order." I turned and then a gal I just knew that I knew from somewhere was right in front of me, brimming with good news.

"It's me, Cheryl," she said, and it suddenly all came back. She looked shorter because this time I was in boots with three inch stacked heels instead of sneakers. "I just had to tell you, I'm graduating from Marquette this weekend with a double major, and it's all because of you!"

Huh? We swapped essentials in a hurry, because I had to get back to the conference and my boss was driving and while he's a terrific guy, he's never been known for his patience. But … she really wasn't kidding.

We'd been soccer moms together many years before, with kids in preschool and grade school, and then had run into each other by chance a few years earlier while I was running an errand at law school. She was working at the university. We hadn't seen each other in years, and as we walked and talked one day on campus and caught up on what our kids were doing, she told me she was tied up in knots about whether she should start taking classes toward a college degree as long as she could get free tuition through her job at the university. She could think of a million reasons that it would be too hard, too inconvenient for everybody else in the family, too complicated. And, of course, she was "too old."

I—keeping in mind that one of the ways that I juggled law school with four kids at home was to remember that in a pinch I could always buy clean socks and underwear at Wal-Mart—urged her to go for it. But the argument that clinched the deal, apparently, was something my long-departed grandmother had told my Aunt Patsy years ago when Aunt Patsy was agonizing over whether to go back to school and study accounting.

Grandma was a poorly educated but quick witted and tart-tongued Irish immigrant with a very practical bent. "You're going to be fifty years old whether you have that accounting degree or not. So why don't you turn fifty with it?" My aunt took that encouraging ass-kicking advice, got her C.P.A., and rapidly made life hell for tax cheats, working for the I.R.S. I will always remember the story. And so, apparently, will Cheryl.

We laughed and hugged each other at the diner, and then I left. My head was spinning for a long time, and it had nothing to do with trying to fold my five-foot-ten-in-heels frame into the back of the Jeep. It had everything to do with the power of a kind word and a little encouragement, and what had brought me this far.

I sometimes think that we're all just in the middle of a giant three-dimensional pinball machine, thrown from one trajectory to another by things entirely unpredictable. But one thing that remains constant is the remarkable power of believing in someone, and telling them about it. You just never know where that's going to end up.

For me, serendipity threw me off the full-time mommy track and on the path to law school at a tourist bar in Florida. I was on vacation with my two year old son and some relatives on Sanibel Island, and had arranged to have lunch with a guy I hadn't seen in seventeen years but knew from when I was a college sophomore. We reconnected because of a reunion newsletter. He was working in Florida, and so one day he drove across the state via "Alligator Alley" and we caught up. Umpteen years earlier, he'd been a really bright, challenging, dissatisfied and angry young man, and dropped out (or been kicked out, I was never quite sure) of college. I had thought his potential was limitless, and before he left I bought him a poster to take with him. It said "If you set your sights among the heavens, even if you fail, you will fall among the stars."

Seventeen years later, he had long since pulled his act together, gone back to school, become a highly accomplished federal attorney. We covered a lot of ground over chicken sandwiches and fries and diet Cokes. I jerked his chain and told him I thought he'd be a terrific writer. He jerked mine and told me he thought I'd be a really good lawyer. I was happily writing a novel, and didn't think I had the brain power to possibly consider such a leap. He wasn't buying it. He never had. "What, you think you're too old to change?" he shot back.

I went back home, mulled the challenge, took the LSAT to see if my brain still worked, got accepted to law school and started making the place my own. In the early days, if I hit a questionable patch, I reminded myself that John believed I could do this, shut my eyes, and forged ahead. Eventually I came to believe more in myself, and didn't need his faith to fall back on. But I was glad to have had it when I started.

So I often tell my kids that kindness is never wasted. That if you have something good to say about someone, say it sooner rather than later because you just never know what shores that encouragement will carry them to.

Just ask John. Or Cheryl. Or Aunt Patsy. Or me.

Gone Fishin'

My youngest son eased the SUV backward down the shallow mud slope, putting the wheels of the trailer a few feet into the water. The channel leading to the lake seemed not much wider than the row boat, and I stood a few feet to the side, out of the way and out of trouble. I was in thoroughly unfamiliar territory, both metaphorically and literally—I had absolutely no idea where we were. Not that it mattered, since for the next few hours, I was entirely in his hands. It had to happen some day.

We were there on the edge of his favorite lake, putting an aluminum rowboat into the water, at my suggestion. Begging, in fact. Fishing had taken hold of Robert with a vengeance this summer, coinciding with the triumph of getting his driver's license and being able to haul a boat and a trailer behind his small SUV. I had soon turned a little envious of his water-borne adventures with his high school buddies.

Okay, the part about getting up at five in the morning for a good start didn't hold any charm for me. But in overhearing snatches of conversation here and there, I formed the wistful impression of hours spent soaking in the grandeur of nature, sunrises, sunsets, loons, ducks, occasional fish caught and released, moonlit excursions under star-studded skies that involved more relaxing and talking about life and politics than actually fishing but still sounded heavenly.

And so I bugged him to take me fishing on one of the last mornings before school started up again. We set a date and hoped for good weather. At the appointed Mom-friendly hour, I drove up to the house bearing bug spray, sunblock, and nice 'n' greasy McDonald's breakfasts for the both of us. Climbed into the front passenger seat, and settled in for the ride. He'd been busy already, industriously packing fishing rods, tackle boxes, a cooler full of drinks, nets, a carton of juicy nightcrawlers, and life jackets.

This was definitely his show. He competently pushed the boat off the trailer, parked the SUV, and held the boat steady for me to climb into. We poled our way off the mud bottom and down the channel until the boat started to float on its own, then paddled through an ocean of shiny green lily pads fringed by rushes and tall grass. The last of the lily pads finally behind us, we floated out into wide open spaces. Only a few feet deep, and tiny in comparison to other recreational lakes in our county, this pond nonetheless had rustic charm to spare. Only a few houses ringed its shoreline—nature reigned supreme. Too shallow for larger boats and "personal watercraft," too difficult for access for more than the true die-hards who didn't mind getting muddy to get there, this was a lake for those few who REALLY treasured peace and quiet and, dare I say it, utter serenity.

Great blue herons, standing four feet tall on long twig-like legs, spread their six-foot silver wings and floated along the perimeter of the lake, slow and measured wing-beats indicating no hurry, no worries. Their necks arched back in graceful S-curves, and narrow heads perched regally above their chests, their long legs trailing behind like a ballerina's arabesque. Unseen but still present, sandhill cranes clacked musically from the sidelines, and Canada geese passed, honking, overhead. A pair of ducks shot airborne across the lake, all speed and business, like turbo-charged Mini Coopers compared to the herons' languid touring cars.

Wind riffled the crystilline water's surface, and we passed over forests of strange vegetation below, some plants with leaves curled upwards like submarine calla lilies, others with riots of long, furry arms reaching upwards and crossways, chenille yarn for fish and mermaids to fantastically knit. A damselfly perched casually on my knee, and I let him sit, undisturbed. The weather was perfect. Sunny, no clouds above but a small handful scattered at the horizons. Light wind, enough to both keep us cool and move the boat, but not enough to rock it.

He set me up with a casting rod, starting with the basics: an earthworm on a hook, with a plastic bobber attached to let me know if a fish started to nibble. Later in the morning I graduated to an artificial lure and left the bobber behind in favor of the thrill of the chase. He upgraded to a "buzz" lure, hoping to land a northern. I surprised my son—nice to still be able to do that every so often—by casting respectably from the get-go. All those hours spent horse-training decades ago, lightly cracking a long-handled whip to snap the air just behind my gelding's haunches as he dutifully trotted in circles around me, were good for something.

We sat, and drifted, and casted, and occasionally motored to new spots, and detangled our lines from the weeds they snagged in. We landed four feisty bass, two apiece. I marveled at how beautiful of a day we'd lucked out with. And I marveled, too, at how lovely it is when the roles get reversed, and I could sit back and enjoy the ride.

There's inevitably a tipping point—or there should be—when you look at the kid you have raised from day one, through diapers and ear infections and teething and bruises and homework and late-night trips to the E.R., piano recitals and back-to-school shopping and driver's ed, and realize that they can do some stuff on their own.

For my older son, that moment came when he was eighteen and I flew to Germany to visit him for a weekend. He was spending several months there as a foreign exchange student. I not only spoke no German, I barely knew which end of the country he was living in. I'd started listening to a "German for Dummies" CD in the airport lounge before takeoff from Chicago, then gave up twenty minutes later. Too late to pick up the language then. So for four days a few thousand miles from home, I took all my cues from my son.

He navigated the trains, gave me a walking tour around the neighborhood and the town center, picked a café where we had coffee and ice cream, warned me to keep my purse closer to me when we sat so it would be out of pickpocket range, navigated all the signs and directions and bathrooms and menus, and translated more than adequately at an impromptu gathering of my German cousins before we left.

For my oldest daughter—the "training baby" we mother's have the hardest time cutting the apron strings on—the moment came watching her as she addressed a crowd of about twenty five hundred students from an auditorium stage at a convention she'd helped to plan. For the younger one, it came at the end of a long day at the office, a hundred fifty miles of highway under my belt, and an awards banquet we'd attended that evening where she'd received a scholarship. As I sat on living room sofa of her new student apartment, the "guest room" where I would sleep the night in comfort just ten feet away and her cat watching warily from the sidelines, she kicked into maternal comfort mode. Let me get you a cup of tea, she suggested. Would I like to watch "Sex and the City?" I put my feet up on the coffee table and accepted my new place in the world. It felt good. And now it was that time for my "caboose baby."

Three hours after Robert and I first poled and paddled our way out to the middle of the lake, it was time to make our way home. He expertly located the tiny break in the identical stands of tall grass rimming the lake, and navigated us back up the channel to the spot where we'd left the car. Grunting and struggling mightily, he wrestled the boat—usually a two man job—by inches on to the back end of the trailer. I stayed out of the way as he balanced on the trailer and manhandled the full load, then tentatively worked the winch at his direction when the time came. Gear unloaded and boat buckled down, we slowly made our way home and back to reality and routine. "Thanks honey," I said, "this was just … beautiful!"

The school year has started, the house is again quiet, and autumn is settling in. A few sugar maples have started to brilliantly catch fire and drop their leaves already, signaling an encroaching end to long days spent outdoors in shorts and sandals. There's no more talk about the need to get up at five in the morning to get that boat in the water. I can already anticipate breaking out my snowshoes after a good blizzard this winter, and we haven't had the first frost yet.

The march toward the dead of winter is inexorable, with fixtures of hot chocolate, snowdrifts, crackling fires and frosty windshields on the horizon. But no matter how cold it gets, and no matter how few hours of daylight we have for months on end, it won't take much to get my mind back in that boat. If you see me with a far-off stare and a smile on my face this winter as the winds howl outside and the snowflakes fall like cotton, chances are … I've "gone fishin'."

Cookie Therapy

From a distance, I didn't have much to complain about. I was stretched out on one end of a comfy recliner sofa, cat curled up behind me on the bay window sill, new car in the garage, tummy full from dinner, good job, good friends, solid roof over my head, you know the drill. And then, despite the doors and windows and tight screens ... the past crept in, without knocking.

My youngest son sat on the far edge of the recliner, the golden glow of the floor lamp falling on him as he read. The television was on, and he was surrounded by books and folders, pens and papers. He nestled in, intently digging in to the first semester of his junior year. The biggest change for him this year is that now he's driving himself to school.

They say—whoever "they" are—that your past often comes back to haunt you when your children turn the same age that you were when life sideswiped you and left you careening down a different path than the one you knew the week before.

This was my "caboose" baby, the last of the lot, sitting here studying, blissfully unaware at the age of sixteen of his mother's sudden, stumbling trip down memory lane. When his siblings were older and hit that milestone, I was too busy to notice. One, then another, then another turned sixteen, and I kept the plates spinning in the air with little time for reflection. Soccer games, tennis meets, football helmets, potluck dinners, practices, homework, ear infections, summer camps, tests, prom dress shopping, family vacations at the shore. Introspection ... who had the time?

I did now.

Whatever had passed for "normal" as I was growing up in Chicago—traffic noise, Catholic school uniforms in various plaids, city bus schedules, homework, science fairs, French club, knowing that the bed you went to sleep in would still be there a month later—went out the window when I was sixteen. I came home from a six-week study trip to Europe with my high school history teacher and a busload of classmates between sophomore and junior year to find that my parents had gone off the reservation and moved to an abandoned farm in northern Wisconsin, property they had bought a few years earlier "as an investment." I don't remember moving, I don't remember leaving the city, I don't remember arriving at the farm. But somehow, I was just there.

The nearest town was two miles away, with a population of 143. I remember a feed mill, a tiny post office, a softball field, a church. It probably had a bar or two, but we didn't mingle much. Our isolation from the larger world was near total: no television, no newspapers, no newsmagazines, only two channels on the radio—country/western and NPR. The red brick house was missing a front porch and had no indoor plumbing but for a kitchen sink. The place hadn't been lived in for years, and it appeared that the window on the north side of the kitchen had once served as a garbage chute into the yard. They bought two calves and a pony before we built fences. We spent a lot of time chasing them from the open fields back to the barn.

They ordered a couple of dozen chicks from the feedmill, and we raised a flock of Leghorn hens and a pair of roosters. In summer, two of the hens—never say these birds weren't smart—casually loitered like delinquents near the kitchen door and then dashed in when it opened to steal food from the dog's dish. Occasionally they made it as far as the butter dish on the kitchen table before they were scooped up and unceremoniously tossed back outside, fluffing their feathers in indignation. When the weather turned colder, the chickens moved from the coop into the barn with the cow and the horses. When it got really cold and the points of their red combs started to turn black with frostbite, the chickens moved into the basement.

With a hundred untilled acres at our disposal and a father who had grown up in a small German farming village, we cut hay with a scythe and turned it over with a pitchfork. I put a flat tire on the three-quarter ton pickup when I inartfully tried to back it up the ramp to the top of the barn, truck bed filled with a mound of loose, fragrant hay, and steered a little too close to the edge. The wheel rim cut into the soft rubber, and the tire went flat. We finally started buying hay in bales.

When the water pipes froze in the barn in winter, watering the animals started with filling five gallon pails of water in the basement of the house, toting them up the stairs to ground level, then navigating the slippery, snow-covered slope downward from the house, trying not to slosh. The menagerie grew in fits and starts—geese, ducks, a pig, a horse, a Guernsey cow named "Queenie." She had long, curvy horns that scared me to death.

We bought a calf at an auction and brought her home in the back seat of the 1973 yellow Matador. We called her "Daisy." She didn't live all that long. I learned to milk the cow by hand the day she arrived, bucket between my knees, teetering on a tiny stool. We strained the milk through cheesecloth right into glass grape juice bottles and then into the fridge.

I managed to finish another year of high school through all the chaos, and then graduated at the end of my junior year. Stayed on the farm for another year, working occasionally, shoveling mountains of manure, and baking a lot. Pound cakes, layer cakes, white bread, wheat bread, chocolate chip cookies, cinnamon loaves with creamy white frosting. I kneaded the yeast dough to satiny, elastic balls on the wooden kitchen table, the ebb and flow of the rhythm soothing in the midst of all other hardships. I even tried my hand at making raised donuts, frying them in hot goose grease (yes, **those** geese) and then rolling them in sugar. They didn't taste bad.

Time passed. I eventually made my way to college, got a degree, got married, started a family. And kept on baking. I'm from that generation that remembers those Poppin' Fresh Pillsbury Dough Boy commercials and can still sing the jingle, *"**Nothin' says lovin' like something from the oven, and Pillsbury says it best!**"* And I still firmly believe that a little home bakery can make just about anything better.

As the kids grew, I put this standard into practice often. Left with an hour before the school bus dropped them off, I would survey the clutter and weigh my options. I could straighten up the living room before they walked in, sure that any superficial neatness would begin to naturally unravel as soon as they arrived, or I could reach for the chocolate chips. It was a no brainer. Nothing could compare to the sound of the front door opening, a footfall or two and the "thunk" of a school bag hitting the floor, then a tiny pause followed by the rapturous exclamation, "Oooooooh, you made *COOKIES*!!"

Back in the present, after a few days of brooding and feeling strangely bereft of my moorings, I knew it was definitely cookie time. I got out the hand mixer, the chocolate chips, the butter, the vanilla, the eggs. Someone gave me an expensive, heavy KitchenAid stand mixer once, a wondrous, gigantic appliance that could perfectly blend all the ingredients for me while I saved time elsewhere in the kitchen. I used it twice, then moved it permanently to the basement.

There is a primitive, tactile joy in pushing the ingredients around in the bowl, watching the raw materials blend and swirl and transform in stages into the finished product, texture and color changing as each egg or square of melted chocolate or cup of sugar is factored in and combined into the whole. Not unlike building a sand castle, or driving a bulldozer on a construction site, measuring your progress by the way the mound of dirt you're pushing around changes shape. If you could operate it by remote control, well, where's the fun in that?

I mixed, I scraped, I cheated and ate the dough raw from the bowl. I dropped spoonfuls of chocolate-chip-laden dough on cookie sheets and watched them zealously as they baked, whisking them out of the oven precisely when their edges turned light brown and their crowns started to look slightly crisp. My son cruised through the kitchen, and began to graze while they were still warm. I divided up the rest into plastic storage containers—some for us, the rest for the older two I was planning to see the next day.

I picked up the college kids, took them out to lunch, visited, caught up on school and life, strong-armed one into buying shoes. Brought out the home-baked offerings, love neatly sealed in square Ziploc containers. And again, that satisfying, familiar moment of recognition, that happy "Oooooooh … you made *COOKIES*!!"

I feel so much better already.

Bunny Blues

I miss the Easter Bunny.

To be perfectly precise, I miss being the Easter Bunny. And Santa Claus. And the Tooth Fairy. I miss the whole "Easter Theater" and "Christmas Theater" quality of it all, the behind-the-scenes planning, the skullduggery, the hiding places, the fear of being found out. But most of all I miss being the Easter Bunny.

Let's face it, being the Tooth Fairy didn't have a lot of emotional payback. Two minutes of "oh look what the Tooth Fairy left me" was kind of a paltry reward to balance out the fear of discovery as I tiptoed into the bedroom to make the tooth-for-money swap, the circles under my eyes the next morning from staying up late enough to make sure the kid was asleep, and the anxiety over worrying that I'd fall asleep and forget to play my part. (I did forget once, but covered the lapse by going back to my daughter's bedroom to help search one more time and accidentally "finding" the dollar that had "fallen" between the bed and the wall. Good save, eh?)

Christmas with little kids around of course is the Sistine Chapel of maternal deception and orchestration, the prime example of why I've long said that one of the qualities of being a really good mother is the ability to lie like a rug. Approximately two months of planning and shopping and hiding and wrapping and decorating and, closer to the big day, ornament hanging and cookie baking and "Secret Santa" shopping for school buddies and last minute presents for teachers and calendar juggling for family get-togethers. Acres and acres of emotional payback—just feel the warmth of that crackling fire, watch the tinsel glitter and gleam when the tree and a few candles are the only things lit in the living room—in exchange for a time commitment something akin to planning the Normandy invasion.

But Easter, ah! Religious origins and overtones aside, a holiday devoted simply to the pursuit of chocolate bunnies and chocolate eggs and jelly beans and the riotous fun to be had when a half dozen people sit around the kitchen table vying for the most creative ways to dye and decorate a bunch of hard-boiled eggs. Pastel plaid has always been my favorite.

With my youngest now approaching sixteen, taller than me, and getting into the pole position for taking his driver's license test in a couple of months, I haven't had any true believers around the house for quite a while. Although for a few years after the youngest finally got clued in on the game, I still had even the college kids in their pajamas running around the yard looking for plastic eggs on Easter morning … and pealing with laughing while they did.

To my credit, my "caboose baby" actually made it to ten before I finally lowered the reality boom. It would have been tempting to see how long I could keep it up—his older siblings were all gamely in on the deal—but the day after Easter that fateful year was going to be his first day of baseball practice. I foresaw him showing up on the playing field happily sharing "oh, this is what the Easter Bunny left for me!" and then the older guys on the team would just eat him alive.

So, reluctantly, I took a deep breath that morning, steeled myself, and fessed up. I was the Easter Bunny. And the Tooth Fairy too. He seemed to take the news in stride and walked off. But he came back a few minutes later as I was fixing my hair in the bathroom, his eyes wary.

"You'd better not be Santa Claus too!" Oooooooohhhhhh, now the jig was really up.

For roughly the next six months, even more, I could see that his universe had shifted to absorb the magnitude of the truth and the scope of the life-long trickery. He'd hold up a favorite toy, game, book with a mixture of discovery and reproach. "So this came from you and not from Santa Claus?" Huh. Maturity's a hard thing to watch evolve.

Though he didn't let his newfound enlightenment interfere with his glee the next Easter at egg decorating again and searching for his Easter basket before church and combing the yard with the older kids for his share of the treats hidden there.

Easter for the past couple of years has been a bit more subdued, the Easter Bunny noticeably absent. Last year I took the boys to Germany with my father over the Easter break. The year before that was the year of the divorce and new arrangements. This year I'll be in Ireland with the youngest, traveling around for a week and visiting with my cousins. I'll still leave the baskets behind, chock full of chocolate, but it's just not the same. Children living away from home and over the age of being hoodwinked are one thing, but even the cats have taken their toll on the holiday in that time too.

The centerpiece of Easter decorating had long been my "Easter tree," which sat in the living room window, hung with fragile eggs I'd blown and hand-painted back in the day when I baked a lot more cookies and read bed-time stories and still watched "Sesame Street" with the kids. I haven't brought the Easter tree out of hiding since we got the first kitten two years ago—I've seen what that demented maniac does just with Christmas tinsel—and certainly not since the retriever has come late to the realization that the sill in the bay window is a fine place from which to stand and bark at the world when I'm not at home.

Life's very good right now, even though none of the Easter toys have come out of the box yet this year. All the kids and I will get to happily reconnect at my niece's wedding soon, and share in the optimism of new beginnings. I have great kids, great friends, a great job, and after a couple of near-death experiences, I'm still appreciatively walking around freely on my own steam and swinging a hand saw or a cordless drill on occasion. Nothing really to complain about when you look at it …

But … DAMN I still miss the Easter Bunny!

Spellbound in Hibernia

The rain and the centuries had long washed the blood from the rocks under our feet, but the echoes of history and voices long-stilled hung in the air like the smoke from a peat fire.

From atop the Rock of Dunamase, a craggy ruined fort last sacked by Oliver Cromwell's forces in 1650, the plains of County Laoise fell away into a patchwork of green and gold under an impossibly sunny sky. It was the kind of picture perfect weather the Irish Tourist Board might post on a website to lull travelers and other hopeless optimists into thinking the Emerald Isle gets more than four or five days without rain in a year. My teenaged son and I had the fort virtually to ourselves on this morning, and we climbed and clambered to our heart's content over ruined stone walls and the spongy grass in between.

This place was marked in the guidebooks as a stop worth making, but for a change all was still. There were no ticket takers here, no ice cream stands, no public toilets, postcards, gift shops, guided tours. We missed the tiny road sign the first time we drove past. And nearly missed the road again when we doubled back.

There was only silence broken by trilling of birds in the surrounding fields, the aroma of green grass mixed with the smell of crumbling rock, an eagle's eye view down hillsides which had seen attackers—from Vikings in the tenth century to Cromwellian soldiers in the seventeenth-climb brutally upward to seize the high ground. Several long, vertical "arrow loop" windows still remained, and it didn't take much to imagine drawing swiftly down with a longbow in times when lives were far shorter and mettle was tested up close and personal.

There is much about Ireland that leaves me entranced, a great deal of it to do with the fact that over there, I'm connected to a far-flung tribe of wonderful cousins who all talk even faster than I do. Talk about validation!! Conversations tumble and overlap like creeks and rivulets splashing into a trout stream, words pouring forth with a teasing joy of connection and not a little delightful and affectionate one-upmanship. Ah, bliss!

And the profound joy that resonates every time I return to my grandfather's home town of Templetuohy and sit in the kitchen of the old house, remembering visits past and tea and toast with Aunt Maggie as the turf glowed and crackled in the kitchen stove. "Feel your roots, honey," I told my son as we stretched out on the warm grass in the graveyard beside the family plot, just up the street from the house, in his first visit to Ireland.

But a good measure of the enchantment has to do with the way that history is still alive there. Perhaps it's because it's been less than a century since Ireland threw off Britain's heavy yoke, and the centuries of conflict and desolation that prefaced the nation are still within easy shouting distance and dinner table conversation. And perhaps its because every time you turn around, over your shoulder you'll see yet another castle or crumbling, abandoned stone tower in a cow pasture, a reminder that the progress of peoples and nations is written in loss and anguish and bittersweet victory, and the opening of another fungible shopping mall on a landscape of concrete isn't necessarily the be-all of human accomplishment. Even if you CAN get your favorite Starbucks coffee ("with whip!"), some snazzy wine glasses, and a cute skirt on sale within a hundred feet of each other.

Seriously, when was the last time you heard a political argument on this side of the pond couched in language of grievance about the latest ham-fisted arrogance of King George in the years leading up to the Revolutionary War? Or had any reason to discuss whether Abraham Lincoln had help in drafting, say, the Gettysburg Address ... and how the writer was possibly connected to your family.

And yet, in the tiny fishing town of Passage East in Ireland's southeast, it seemed somehow not out of keeping at all for aggrieved local fisherman, bitterly protesting a ban on salmon drift-netting, to post signs drawing stinging comparisons between the current prime minister and Oliver Cromwell's brutal campaign of suppression four hundred years apart. And have the prime minister come out the worst. Or to sit at the dinner table at my cousin's house in County Clare on the other side of the country and casually discover a six-degrees-of-separation link between my family and a member of the gentry who had helped the "Liberator of Ireland," Daniel O'Connell, craft some of his speeches in the 1800s. And could you pass the butter, please? Peggy, the barbecued salmon is absolutely delicious! Please, tell me more! It doesn't seem that long ago …

Under a sunny sky at Dunamase, classrooms and courtrooms and shopping malls were literally worlds away. There were no judges, no lawyers, no telephones, no teachers, and no coaches to break in on our feeling of discovery, and our moments of reverie. Just a steep and precarious walk upwards into the past. And the feeling, however short, of being absolutely spellbound.

The Gatorade Reality Check

The Gatorade was officially called "Wild Berry," but it was a gorgeous, most unberry-like deep azure blue. Like a swath of the Caribbean staring back at you from a glossy travel poster beckoning you in the dead of winter to warmer climes with powdery white sand beaches, and fruity drinks with little umbrellas, and, just maybe, a cabana boy or two to ogle. Or like those "blue raspberry" popsicles with the two sticks you bought at the corner store when you were a kid, hoping that you could slurp them down on a steaming summer day before they melted and dripped blue stains all over your clothes.

Yes, the Gatorade was pretty under any other circumstances, but it was now pooling in the middle of a Laura Ashley bedspread, and a friend of my son's who had just spilled it entirely by accident in the room she was bunking in was sheepishly repeating "I'm sorry, I'm so sorry, I'm so sorry about this!" as I kicked into emergency mode and ripped the covers off the bed.

She was mortified, and I was scrambling, and my biggest priority at that exact instant was to keep this deluge of vivid blue from soaking through to the mattress. I made it by a whisker. "Is there anything I can do," she continued, "I'm so sorry, I've got another comforter along, I'm so sorry!"

I told her not to worry, and the kids soon left to go out to dinner as planned. They threw the bedding into the back of my car for me, and I followed with a bottle of detergent and several bucks worth of quarters on my way to the Laundromat. And on the way there, in the cold and the dark, I reminded myself of what was really important in life and why I didn't really give a rip about whether the very pretty comforter set was ruined. It had already done what it needed to do.

I'm not a person whose house has many luxury touches. My kitchen cabinets are the same particle board with plastic veneer that I moved my pots and pans into twenty five years ago when we first built. Half the carpeting has been replaced—but the other half is still the original stuff, and shows every day of its age. The living room hasn't been painted in about fifteen years. But one day about six months ago, I felt the need to buy a twin-sized Laura Ashley comforter and sheet set on the spot and bring it home.

It's gorgeous. The comforter is a rich seafoam green and cream brocade, far too plump to ever fit in my own washing machine, ruched and quilted and heavy and … well … comforting. The sheets I bought to go with are light shell pink, showered with pink cabbage roses in various stages of bloom and dark green leaves evoking the carefree, mythic abandon of Marie Antionette playing shepherdess at Versailles. And I bought them because my daughter had cancer.

She's completely, thankfully fine now, but life can change in a heartbeat. All of ours had a month earlier, when she called to say that she had been unexpectedly diagnosed with thyroid cancer. Ten days before that I'd been sitting on a bar stool in a crowded yuppie bar in the Twin Cities after midnight, a buzz on from the drinks had earlier in the evening, buying for both my daughters and celebrating the older one's graduation from law school the next day. We felt like we had the world by the tail. Less than two weeks later, I was getting ready to leave my office, peeling out of my spike heels, showing off pictures of the graduation ceremony to a friend in uniform, when my ex-husband called to tell me that my "training baby" had cancer. Bam, we entered a new universe.

A frenzy of shock and concern and activity followed, as doctors were auditioned and surgery was scheduled and insurance was navigated. Work was rescheduled and plans were made to travel to the hospital and stay as long as any of us were needed. But before that, I hastily pulled together a graduation party for her (law school) and her younger brother (high school) on the only weekend before the surgery that we could all get together as a family. And if she was coming home, she was going to need a place to settle in for a few days.

This was no small task. She'd lived away from home for most of the past seven years, in the state next door throughout her undergraduate degree and then during law school. Over the past year I'd turned her tiny bedroom—large enough for a desk and a dresser and a twin bed but nothing bigger—into a storage closet after the divorce as I dug out the master bedroom, repainted, hung lace curtains, reorganized. It took me three days to just get the extra stuff out of her room, move it temporarily back into mine, and dust and vacuum the room from top to bottom. And handle a last-minute felony drunk-driving trial as well.

And then I went shopping. It wasn't a rational, planned, shop-the-sales-and-just-be-practical kind of trip. It was a visceral, instinctive, primordial drive fueled by the thought that my baby was in trouble, and she needed a soft nest to land in. And Laura Ashley was just the thing. The room looked stunning when I got done, far nicer than when she'd ever lived at home.

We spent the next three days squeezing in as much togetherness as we could. We went to dinner, we went shoe shopping, we had the graduation party complete with a festive cake from the best bakery in town, we ate burgers and onion rings and sundaes outdoors at the local custard stand. I baked banana muffins, made coffee, got out fresh towels, hovered. She slept in late all three days, burrowed into those pretty flowered sheets and brocade coverlet. And then, at the end of the weekend, she went back to the Twin Cities to get the rest of her work and surgery arrangements in order, and I finally sat down and let myself fall apart for a little while.

The Laura Ashley set is now back on the bed, all traces of Gatorade washed down the drain at the Laundromat, ready for the next houseguest. I was quite surprised. I thought that Caribbean ocean blue was set for the long haul, just another small reminder that life never goes smoothly, and if you expect that it will, boy are you in for some rude awakenings.

But if it had, I wouldn't have blinked an eye.

A Tale of Two Kitties

The Bride of Frankenstein is moving in with me. She's already here, in fact, she just doesn't know she won't be leaving in another week or so.

She was my last big surprise of 2006. On New Year's Eve, as I stood making light conversation at a party in Milwaukee, wine glass in hand, cashmere sweater sparkling, perky bows on my killer spikes, feelings of warmth and good cheer and "whew, we made it!" in abundance. All enhanced by the anticipation of the lobster dinner still ahead, and the platter of "death by chocolate" brownies I'd brought to share for dessert. With three and a half hours to go until the year turned over, the Packers were ahead 13-0 in the football season's last game over the Chicago Bears, and after a turbulent year, it finally looked like smooth sailing the rest of the way until midnight. I was feeling very mellow. That's always a bad sign in the cosmos.

That was right about the time when my younger daughter showed up at her apartment in Madison and found a note from her landlord on the door with an ultimatum: if there's a cat in the place, either lose the cat or lose the lease. A desperate cell phone call later from child to parent, and my universe instantly expanded to include a spare cat. Oh goody!! Twice the cat hair, twice the litter boxes, twice the reproach in the old dog's eyes over being displaced yet again.

Mooka, a/k/a the Bride of Frankenstein, is exquisite. Five and a half pounds of slender, perfectly proportioned sinuous feline grace. Wrapped in a short-haired tabby coat of feral taupes and greys and black and cream with the shiny feel of sealskin. Tiny little paws that could be the model for Carl Sandburg's poetic fog that "comes on little cat feet."

You look at this dainty, mysterious, self-possessed little predator, and you understand completely why the Egyptians worshipped cats. In silhouette, ears pitched forward as she sits, motionless, regarding the rest of the world from the edge of the kitchen table, she resembles nothing less than a statue of the Egyptian cat goddess Bastet carved in stone and standing sentinel in a pyramid at Giza.

Trouble is, another cat already owns my house. That would be Smokey. Smokey joined us as a tiny ten week old kitten nearly two years ago and now thuds around on ham-sized paws at sixteen pounds, prowling like a small bear twice that size under his poofy long hair. Judging by his skill at catching mice—and his generosity at displaying them to me as a token of his affection—he is quite a mighty hunter himself.

He is a "tuxedo cat," velvety black with magnificent white paws that look like he dipped them in a bowl of heavy cream, snowy white chest and belly, and a white Elizabethan ruffed collar. His movements stalking are perfect, precise, patient beyond belief. But the fluffy coat just kills the dramatic effect. It's as though you took Daniel Craig, the fabulously buff new cinematic James Bond, and set him at a casino table in Monte Carlo in a tuxedo made entirely of marabou feathers. Might as well put him in a clown suit with a blinking red nose. Still, Smokey ruled the roost—and Bandit, the chocolate lab—with confidence and authority. The spare cat has put that world right on end.

You could definitely say that this pair has "chemistry." The same kind Elsa Lanchester had for Boris Karloff in the 1935 movie "The Bride of Frankenstein" when the monster's bride—draped in white and sporting a pre-Marge Simpson up-do—was brought to life and finally unveiled to meet her badly-stitched suitor. It didn't go well then (the bride's reaction has been called "one of the most famous screams in screen history"), and it didn't go well now. And both these kids have all their original claws.

We had a preview of this transition last Christmas, when Mooka came home for the holidays for the first time. It started with a lot of hissing and growling and stalking, circling, watching, waiting, pouncing, and ended days later with blood splatters on the kitchen floor. We lived through it—though I cringed the day I saw Mooka's claws stretching one of Smokey's eyelids as the pair awkwardly tried to separate after a brief skirmish.

All's quiet on the battlefront right now, the fighters have retired to the safety of their respective floors of the house. Smokey prefers to hang out in the laundry room, from his perch on the bin full of Easter decorations. When she's not hanging out in my daughter's bedroom, full of familiar scents, Mooka likes the safety of one of my closets. At the moment, there are no blood-curdling screams, no "don't mess with me" warning growls, no wondering whether it's safe to blindly reach under the bedskirt for a pair of shoes without risking severing an artery. But like all truces and DMZs still in under construction, I know it's too early to last.

I'll just keep the paper towels handy. And the vet on speed dial.

Return to the Fatherland

The sleek black Mercedes sedan devoured the autobahn under our tires, purring like a contented panther in high gear as the countryside flew past spotless tinted windows.

"Nicht so schnell!" Not so fast. My father's voice was querulous beside me, a reminder that even if I was driving a car that felt and handled a lot like a jet, I didn't get to push the limits. At least not when he was in the front passenger seat. The speed of the cars passing us in the left lane like the Blue Angels made him nervous, but there was much else to adjust to. For all of us.

My father, myself, and my two teenaged sons were flying along the autobahn in Germany just a year ago to reunite my dad with the family he had not seen in twenty five years. Or forty, depending on who in the family you talked to. And we were there because my older son, Michael, had met the relatives a few months earlier while he was a foreign exchange student near Hanover, and left an impromptu but large family gathering absolutely stunned that his grandfather had not seen his sisters in decades.

I had sat with him at the self-same table—understanding not a word of the animated conversation that rapidly swirled around me in German, smiling and nodding and having another glass or wine or slice of cake. I certainly didn't leave the house with the same generous imperative. But from the kindness in his heart and the depth of his conviction that "Mom, I have to fix that!" came an odyssey we could never have expected.

Plans were made to take my father and both of the boys to Germany over the Easter school vacation that followed. Cousins and friends overseas were contacted, tickets bought, a car rented, an itinerary roughed out. There was no question that my father deserved the trip. Only months earlier he had remarked that he would love to return to Germany again before he died. And at eighty two, especially, nobody is guaranteed another sunrise.

His had not been an easy life. He grew up in a farming village in western Germany, happy there until the start of World War II when he was pressed into service, first as an aircraft mechanic and then, as the war ground on, as a foot soldier. His only brother, Ewald, died on the Russian front with a bullet in his head. He himself surrendered after three days in a foxhole outside Aachen under a barrage of Allied shelling. He spent three years as a prisoner of war, much of it in a coal mine in France. Marriage to my American mother brought him to the United States, and his life here translated into a series of hard and dirty factory jobs in Chicago and Wisconsin to support his family. He never did really grasp the English language very well.

My first inkling that my father's health and his mind were not all that they had been came only four days before we left. I had driven the 120 miles to Chicago with my younger son to get passports issued in person for both of them. Yes, I suppose I could have done this by mail, paid an extra "expedited passport" fee to get them processed quickly. But Hurricane Katrina had wreaked its damage on New Orleans and southern Mississippi not that long before, and my faith in the federal government to accomplish anything in a hurry was at rock bottom.

The three of us went down to the passport office in the Kluczynski Federal Building in Chicago's Loop, and I was shocked by the time we arrived. Both by how frail my father had become—his skin was like paper and his bones seemed as tiny as a bird's—and how easily confused he was. He possessed not an ounce of stamina, and we cabbed it rather than walk the four blocks to the Art Institute to kill the processing time before the passports would be ready. After a brief lunch, we drove him back home to the city outskirts and then returned to the Loop to pick up the passports later to spare him the strain.

Still, there was no thought of calling off the trip. The boys and I gamely tag-teamed him as we traversed the maze of O'Hare Field, airport security, the wait in the lounge to board the plane, and finally our seats on the big Lufthansa jet for our non-stop flight to Frankfurt. Once belted into his seat and aloft, my father relaxed. Had a couple of beers with the boys and a good meal. Chatted animatedly with the lady in the next seat who appeared to find him fascinating.

Ten hours later we landed in Frankfort in the early morning, retrieved our luggage, picked up the rental car, and began the long drive to my cousin's house. We stopped for coffee and pastry in some small town along the way, walking ever so slowly down the narrow streets and guiding him like a child away from passing traffic.

Once we arrived at my cousin Ingrid's lovely hilltop home, the festivities were non-stop. My brother and his daughter had come in from Slovenia to join us for a few days, and the entourage grew larger. We spent the afternoon walking through stalls of flower vendors in the village square and viewed old castle walls in Mayen near Koblenz. We went to late evening Mass on Easter Saturday, drinking hot spiced wine around a bonfire by the church afterward.

On Easter Sunday, there was a family reunion at a restaurant in nearby Emmelshausen. As we walked down the street toward the restaurant, my father looking stiffly formal in a navy blazer, an elderly woman and her husband stopped him, dumbfounded. "Is that you, Willie Wagner?" They hailed from his home town, and had not seen him in half a century. He seemed to recognize the woman, and conversed a little with her in German.

After lunch, we drove, en masse, to the village of Doerth where my father had been born and raised. The church had been restored since the war, and we gazed at the stained glass window dedicated to his fallen brother. Through it all he looked exhausted, and I did not leave his elbow unless there was someone else to take my place. There was a feast later, of course, at my aunt's house. The family instantly grasped that my father's lucidity was a "sometime" thing, and fussed over him endlessly, an arm draped across his shoulder, a cup of coffee or a glass of wine offered at his elbow. Conversation crackled around him, full of reminiscence and anecdote and affection. Sometimes he stepped right into the talk, a quick stream of German coming from his lips and a spark of connection in his eyes. And then moments would pass as he sat, statue-like, gazing wordlessly into the past. Or nothing.

The days that followed were filled with joy and activity and excitement. We took a boat trip down the Rhine. Had another family dinner afterward. Photo albums were produced, "Willie, do you remember?" Sometimes he spoke, sometimes he nodded, sometimes he just said nothing. There were times he spoke to me in German, and to his sisters in English. We took him to Trier, parking as close as we could to the Romanesque cathedral so his steps would be as few as possible. We drove right past the coliseum, because stopping to look around would have been more than he could take. When we left my aunt's house after the second big family dinner, there were many emotional goodbyes to be said. He looked at me without recognition, shook my hand, and politely said his farewell.

"No Daddy, it's me, you're going home with me."

The last few days in his native country continued to sap his energy and awareness. We stopped in Cologne to see the cathedral because my father had told me in the weeks before we left that he had never been there and would like to visit. But once inside, he shuffled along at a snail's pace, looking neither left nor right. A one-year-old would have been more responsive, I thought sadly, young and inquisitive eyes drawn instinctively to gleaming brass and brilliant stained glass.

I stopped him from time to time and placed my hands on his shoulders, turning him gently to face the incomparable windows. "Look, Daddy, isn't that beautiful?" He would nod, and then the shuffle would resume. I turned the boys loose for a half hour to climb the cathedral spire, and my father and I sat in silence in one of the pews. Tourists and other faithful meandered around us slowly, awe-struck, always looking up, their eyes drawn to arches and statuary and filigree and biblical stories captured in radiant glassworks. From what I remember, he looked mostly straight ahead.

By the time we left Frankfort, headed again across the Atlantic, my father was ragged. He had been feted and celebrated, guided and pampered every step of the way. But the uncertainty of his surroundings and the strain of travel had taken its toll. As we searched for our seats on the plane, he could not grasp why we could not take the first seats we saw nearby. Where did all these people come from, he asked. Once seated, he thought he was in church. We commandeered a wheelchair for him upon landing, and his grandsons watched him like a hawk while I retrieved the car from the long-term parking lot apparently set in another zip code.

A year later, my father has returned to what passes for "normal" these days. He lets the dog out, make a cup of tea, helps make dinner, listens to the radio. Sometimes he remembers things like the price of chocolate ten years ago, sometimes he forgets to lock the front door behind him. Despite the photo album and videocassette I made of our trip, I don't know how much of it he really remembers.

But I like to think … in fact I need to believe … that the fact that he stepped out of a shiny black Mercedes on Easter Sunday to the cobblestoned streets of his birthplace with two strapping grandsons and a smiling daughter in a polka-dot silk dress somehow … mattered.

And still lingers.

The Closets of Doom

They say Rome wasn't built in a day ... and neither were the "Closets of Doom."

I felt a bit like Frodo Baggins as he set off in the "Lord of the Rings" for the far-away land of Mordor, with death and adventure just over the horizon. Not a clue as to what was really in store, just a sense of foreboding that righteously kept on building.

I had set the Fates in motion by ordering new carpeting just before New Years Day for two bedrooms and four closets. It seemed like a good idea at the time, replacing the last of the original carpeting that was a quarter century old and dated back to day one of the house. It seemed like a particularly good and timely idea, given that I'd ripped a hole in the ball of my foot a few weeks earlier by getting snagged on a tacking strip laid bare by years of regular foot traffic in front of the bathroom. Nothing screams "immediate home improvement" like personal injury and a tetanus shot.

And like Frodo, I had no idea what I was getting in to. I just knew the job would be big. Piles of dust-collecting stuff had to get moved off the floors, beds broken down and mattresses and springs stored sideways in the family room, clothes removed from closets and dumped anywhere but where they belonged. I signed the paperwork on New Years Eve, smiled, and promised to be ready in four days.

Two days later—with one long and expensive visit to the doggie emergency room, the discovery of a giant ice dam under the blanket of snow on my kitchen roof, and the beginnings of the flu—I caved in to reality and rescheduled for a week after. It still nearly killed me, and I still barely made it.

I am a victim of my own bad habits. I have a mixture of methods for cleaning up the place, and none of them is good. The two major ones are the "piling system," and the "hurry company's coming, scoop it off the table, put it in a laundry basket, and I'll look at it tomorrow" system. Judging by the number of piles and the baskets, tomorrow would never come. But all of a sudden, tomorrow was just around the corner, arriving with 100% polyester carpeting, vapor-proof padding, and a team of installers expecting a lot of elbow room. I fought my natural laissez-faire tendencies and got to work.

Cleaning out the closets of course didn't start with the closets. Instead there was a reverse (or you could say perverse) domino effect in play. In order to make temporary room for the stacks and boxes of assorted detritus in the bedrooms and the closets, other areas of the house were going to have to go under the knife.

I started with the bookcase in the living room. Five grocery bags of discarded books later, I set to the task of clearing out every recyclable magazine in the house. They dated back to … well, some of them in untouched drawers and unexplored corners of my universe, dated back twenty five years. I resisted the urge to sit down right there and read those old back copies of "Ireland of the Welcomes" and "National Wildlife." Reached a compromise with my inner packrat by saving just a few for the "read 'em later" pile and pitching the rest. Seventeen pairs of shoes and boots made their way to Goodwill. And then I finally got serious.

With the record albums, extra photos, high school memorabilia, dust bunnies and empty CD cases finally out of the way, the closets were left, yawning, bottomless pits of memorabilia and who knew what else. I tossed and turned for nights in bleak anticipation, overwhelmed by the magnitude of hauling and sifting and winnowing, seized by the same paralyzing dread that sets in with any unfamiliar challenge and the question, "will I make it to the finish line before the deadline?" Hercules tackling the Augean stables had it easy by comparison. Not only could he marshal the forces of nature to help him out, diverting two rivers to tackle the mother of all messy jobs … he didn't have to worry about putting anything back.

Down to the wire, I finally dug in. My older son joined me for part of the adventure, and his sense of wonderment at our assorted finds bordered on the archeological.

Quite the treasure trove revealed itself, like the recesses of Aladdin's cave. As we peeled back the various strata, there were heartwarming markers of family history … and just plain weirdness. Shotgun shells (standard and "high velocity") and an ancient service revolver. My Little Ponies. Beanie Babies. Duck decoys. Embroidery floss in dozens of colors, dating back to a time when aspiring to be a domestic goddess was higher on my to-do list. A note to Santa from my oldest daughter nearly two decades before, asking for Nancy Drew mysteries and Black Stallion books and "lots of surprises!" Fencing foils. A gyroscope. A large rock with a bunny picture painted on it. An Austrian dirndl. Scuba fins and snorkels. A child's dinosaur costume with a four-foot long spiked tail. A jacket left behind by Henri, our French foreign exchange student from the summer before. A twelve-foot molted python skin. A lap loom. A recurve longbow. Bamboo fishing rod. A black and white photo of me taken at the age of twenty-one in college, sitting long-haired and demure in a sundress with a rose in my teeth. Another, from an even earlier time when I was four or five, dressed in a sequined tutu on my grandmother's porch on Hirsch Street in Chicago, kicking my ballet slippered foot over my head.

Little by little, the journey into the "Closets of Doom" took on the warmth of memory, and the dread disappeared like fog under the morning sun. The long Donegal tweed cape? A memento of a month-long trip to Ireland made on a shoestring after I graduated from college the first time. Traveling with a bicycle and a backpack, I'd gone wherever the wind took me around the country, determined to see all I could, sure that I'd never again make my way around with quite such carefree abandon. The Austrian dirndl outfit—white "middy" blouse, red peasant jumper flecked with tiny flowers, striped blue and white apron—dated back to a study trip through Europe with my high school classmates and history teacher. I bought it in Salzburg … and it had accidently shrunk beyond hope of wearing by the time we left Madrid. I'd never wanted to get rid of it.

And the diminutive packs of wooden matches from the "Enchantment Resort" outside Sedona? A reminder that not that long ago I'd fled the state of Wisconsin to celebrate one gloomy mid-winter birthday under sunny blue skies instead. Rather than walking into my office to find a stuffed buzzard perched on the back of my chair and some black balloons to help me "celebrate," my friend Annie B and I went sleeveless and hiked the "Eagle's Nest" trail in Arizona's Red Rock State Park near Sedona, then enjoyed a gourmet lunch at the secluded, luxury resort on the outskirts of Sedona, dining on the patio as the warm sun gleamed off red rock canyons rising starkly above us. We finally returned to her home that evening, to bask in the hot tub next to the pool while sipping margaritas we made with oranges picked in her backyard. A memory worth re-igniting … particularly in the dead of winter.

Bit by bit, twenty five years of assorted memorabilia made its way off the closet floor and either on to higher shelves out of the way or into other rooms, to be condensed and reassembled later. The carpet installers arrived on time in a flurry of Spanish and testosterone and cheerful efficiency, leaving pristine empty rooms with soft surfaces underfoot and the smell of fresh synthetic fibers lingering in the air. Hiding out in my kitchen as they worked, in the few square feet unfilled by displaced furniture and unsorted papers, I finally tackled my Christmas cards two weeks late. The "closets of doom" emptied in time, I could finally relax.

As for eventually getting all that stuff back in the closets? Well … that's beginning to look more and more like Pandora's Box.

Life with Predators

Blood stains in the foyer make such a terrible first impression. I'd like to be a crime novelist as much as the next writer, but even I know that when company comes over, the Windex comes out and the evidence gets hidden under the rug.

I live in ***The Predator Zone.*** One cat and one dog on the inside, countless things with sharp claws and teeth in the woods outside—hawks, falcons, coyotes, mink, foxes, and the occasional feral cat scoping out the bluebird nest boxes. We're not even going to get to the camouflage wearin', compound bow-totin', pheasant and deer huntin' son who parks his portable blind next to my car in the garage, making me scoot sideways into the front seat while packing heels and a tapestry tote bag in the morning. I've still got venison from last year's whitetail sitting in the freezer, waiting to be turned into stew or chili.

Indoors, Smokey the cat holds court as the resident evil genius. He has readjusted and visibly relaxed at being the only feline on the premises, now that my daughter has taken the "spare cat" back to college with her after eight months of sub-letting the litter box. The humans get more attention now, more purring, more lap-sitting, more curiosity now that he's not looking over his shoulder tensely anticipating the next ambush. No more triangulating prey with a competitive partner, no more jockeying for the best bird-watching spot at the bay window.

He rules his fiefdom again with a one-track mind: mice. With the advent of autumn, the white-footed mice outside have again started to migrate indoors through undiscovered cracks, and Smokey is on patrol.

And he proudly displays his conquests with artistic flair that would do Madison Avenue proud. Calculates the human traffic patterns, and then places his meticulously cleaned corpses for maximum admiration. Squarely in the middle of the bathroom doorway, centered on the bone-colored tile. Laid out with funereal splendor on the plush bathroom rug where you stand to brush your teeth in the morning. On the top step leading to the living room. Watch where you step in bare feet in this place!

At times the display has the perverse flavor of live theater, as he drops some tiny misbegotten rodent on the floor beside him, barely alive, with four paws in the air, quivering with shock and waiting for the inevitable coup de grace.

Somehow screaming like a chick in a horror flick has still not gotten old after two years of this sort of creative play. If he had a jewel box and opposable thumbs, I'm sure he'd be presenting his kills even more theatrically. For now we all have to settle for improv. And the knowledge that if he was sixty pounds bigger, he'd have us for breakfast in a heartbeat.

At the other end of the predatory spectrum, a few branches down the family tree from prehistoric wolves, is Bandit, the co-dependent retriever. Also lovingly referred to here as the village idiot. Nine and a half years old, we adopted him as a quivering stray puppy from an animal shelter and discovered later that there are some broken spirits you can't entirely repair.

Bandit has all a standard Labrador's love of chasing things—balls, sticks, cats, and boy you should see the speed he turns on when there's a squirrel involved—and none of the happy-go-lucky spirit that naturally goes with. Once medicated with anti-anxiety drugs and anti-depressants, now just wearing a world-weary Gallic droop, he walks around the house with a look in his eyes of "pet me or I'm going to kill myself!" On the up side, he's never too stand-offish to be petted.

His take on the predatory food chain is not to hunt down a mouse and then kill it, it's to find a dead mouse and then roll in it. Left to his own devices in the cold cruel world, he wouldn't last five minutes. Senior dog chow doesn't grow on trees. At the age of nine and a half—close to seventy in human years—the mind isn't all that it should be anymore, and he has some visible senior moments from time to time. He's developed a taste for anything that's dropped on the floor or been left on the sofa and reminds him of us: used Kleenex, pencils, granola bars still in their foil packages, toothpaste, gum of all flavors, the chocolate my sons and I brought back from Germany in our carry-on luggage and forgot to unpack right away and whisk to safety.

But despite senility and domestication, he has managed to keep an ability to follow a blood trail.

Right to the flower beds.

This year was the first time I'd set to gardening with serious fervor—or any fervor at all—for the past fifteen years. Peonies, roses, coneflowers, feverfew, phlox, coreopsis, butterfly bushes, all took root and flourished remarkably for their first summer. (Okay, so one of the transplanted peonies finally died, I'm sure it'll be back next spring!) But the delphiniums were another story. One day they were growing by leaps and bounds, the next they'd been nibbled down to the ground by neighboring rabbits like fresh spring salad.

I checked around with other gardeners, and my sister-in-law suggested a tried and true idea: dried blood meal. The smell of the stuff would keep the rabbits at bay like garlic repelling vampires. I sped to the garden store, bought a bag of blood meal, sprinkled it like pixie dust around the garden. Felt not unlike like Tinkerbell, d/b/a the "Dried Blood Fairy." The blood meal drew a magic circle around the plants, and the cottontails kept their distance. Unmolested by the rabbits, the delphiniums once again began to grow. But every few days thereafter I noticed that something had been digging by their roots. The plants started to look spindly despite the new health regimen.

The mystery was finally solved one evening when I followed Bandit around the house to hurry him back inside. Attracted by the smell of dried blood, he was industriously digging, trying to find whatever smelly thing naturally lay beneath that he could roll in. He gets a lot more supervision when he's outside now, and my delphiniums have started to look a whole lot healthier again.

When all is said and done, when I need amusement and the occasional heart-thudding ambush, not to mention the blood-curdling screech that comes when he takes his lounge act too close to the kitchen traffic and gets his tail accidentally stepped on, I'll take the cat.

When I need adoration, devotion and pure, uncomplicated companionship, I'll take the dog.

And if I want to keep my delphiniums alive ... I'm putting my money on the rabbits.

End of the Trail

It was not the kind of day I would have picked if I had the choice to make. In a perfect world, we would still have been at home, in a grassy field, with sunlight and warmth, and a light breeze riffling the pasture around us. There would have been wide open space, and a big blue sky, and a few more mouthfuls of tender green grass to tear from the ground and savor.

But it was winter, and I had driven through a blizzard to get to the barn north of town where my two horses had spent the colder months for nearly twenty years. The snow on the unplowed road was easily as deep as the undercarriage of my Subaru. The wind rattled the big barn door behind me, and the snow drove sideways loudly into the metal cladding as the mare reached eagerly for another piece of sliced apple. I'd brought a full bag. I didn't think we'd run out. It was time that was running out instead.

I had had at least one horse in my life since I was sixteen years old. That's when Hoki arrived as a frisky, unbroken six-month old colt. Hoki finally passed on the year before this, frail, most likely senile, and thirty three years old, after a life spent mostly eating, sleeping, and daydreaming whatever horses dream about. Probably clover blossoms and a soft, warm place to lie down. We had had some grand times when we were both quite a bit younger. Babe had made it a pair a few years after that, bought on a whim by my parents and ultimately transferred over to me. I joked often than their only real purpose in life was to be big, expensive lawn ornaments. And I loved to just look at them.

For the past twenty years that the horses spent the warmer months pastured at my house, I'd been up at dawn and sometimes earlier every spring and summer and early fall day, often still in my pajamas, sometimes by flashlight, measuring out horse feed and lately medications, and opening pasture fences. I don't think I'll be taking note of nearly as many sunrises from now on.

The other horse stabled in this small barn, bigger and stronger and, I suspect, meaner, tried to muscle her way into the bulk of the apples. I managed to hoard most of them for Babe anyway. A half-dozen prize-winning Dutch rabbits who shared the barn with the horses, their cages nestled by bales of fragrant hay, watched us warily as I parceled out the apple slices, and wept, and kept repeating the same words as I stroked her shaggy neck, "Baby, it's going to be okay. You're going to be okay." The vet would be there soon. But this time, instead of making things better, we were going to end them.

There was a good deal of irony to the fact that the end of the trail had finally arrived during the first serious blizzard of the season. For years, I'd labeled Babe the "Calamity Jane" of the horse world—anything that could possibly medically go wrong with a horse inevitably did for her. In the years I had taken care of her, I had nursed her through multiple, near-fatal bouts with emphysema, laminitis, and colic. An autoimmune disorder left her prone to eye injuries, and they arrived like clockwork every summer for years. And after each disaster, she had bounced back, defying the odds and sometimes the pessimistic predictions of the vet.

But this was different. She had suffered a knee injury earlier in the year, and while cortisone shots had eased her pain and difficulty for several months, the knee had now deteriorated beyond repair. Walking was now a struggle. She had looked at me only days before with the same plaintive stare I had seen through so many other struggles, the unspoken plea, "make it better." And I knew this time that I could not.

On this day, she was thirty two years old, which was about ninety five in human years. And only three weeks before, at that miraculously old age, she was still staggeringly beautiful. She was a palomino, with languid, blonde, Marilyn Monroe looks. Golden coat and flaxen mane and tail. Big brown come-hither eyes fringed by ridiculous long blonde eyelashes. A curvaceous rump, and gorgeous legs. She was lazy as all get out, and I joked often that she was—like many horses—as dumb as a bag of hammers.

But when she startled, and her head flew up and her haunches coiled, ready for flight, muscular neck arched, nostrils flaring and ears perked forward toward imagined danger, she was still every little girl's fantasy of the absolutely perfect horse.

Now, she was dropping weight by the day. On this day, she was damp and bedraggled from the snow melting on her back, and it was clearly a struggle for her to move. The vet finally arrived, and pulled his Suburban full of gear up to the barn door. Because of the blizzard and the snow drifts piling up, we would need to put her down outside the barn to give the hauler a better chance of reaching her later and carting her away.

There was paperwork to sign, of course, there always is for the big, hard decisions in life. And then some more apples, and a nice shot of really good painkillers for the last walk through the barn door. She followed me, trusting, past the rabbits and over the threshold through the small side door, and we stepped unexpectedly into the sunlight.

For a short while, the snow had stopped, and the wind dropped, and the blue sky peaked through the clouds. We trudged through the glittering snow to the appointed place, and I cried some more as I held her halter fast, and stroked her face while the vet busied himself with his final task. Then the moment came, and she dropped like a stone into a soft, perfect blanket of untouched foot-deep powder. She never took another breath.

She was a trouper. And she was beautiful.

Law & Disorder

The burly blond with the gold chains nestled in his chest hair sits in the stuffy conference room across the wood table, mulling his options. His wife, short, pert, neatly coiffed and crisply dressed, sits beside him, supportive, argumentative, loyal to a fault.

He has been charged with disorderly conduct stemming from a violent evening a month ago when, according to her three-page handwritten statement to police, he scared the hell out of her and roughed her up, making her—at least temporarily—regret the presence of his many guns in their house. She sits in front of me now to explain it away, to put the incident in context, to describe their solid marriage and to express her dismay that the State of Wisconsin would think of holding this wonderful man accountable for his actions that terrifying night.

We are engaged in what's called a "pretrial conference." At this point in a criminal case, the accused or an attorney sits down with a prosecutor to discuss the case and see if it can be settled short of a trial. The options are pretty simple: either accept the state's offer— here a guilty plea in exchange for a recommendation of probation as a first-offender, no gun possession during the probationary period, counseling—or roll the dice and take the case to trial. In this case, a conviction could potentially trigger a federal law barring him from owning guns in the future.

Faced with the possible gun ban, he decides to take his chances with a jury. When all is said and done, he feels that nothing that he did that night violated any law. His wife is equally obstinate. She will not testify against him, period. Women, she states passionately, should become more educated about what unfair consequences could befall their mates if they call 911 during a domestic incident.

I walk them to the conference room door, promise them copies of the police reports, wish them luck. I hope he doesn't kill her when he reads what she wrote down for the police, when the incident was still fresh. I feel like I've gone through the looking glass. But there's no time to think more deeply about it, because it's time to call the next defendant in for a chat.

I am an assistant district attorney for the State of Wisconsin. Welcome to my world. I love my job.

This is my second career. With twenty five years in as a soccer mom and fifteen years spent as a journalist, I am tough to impress. Between this job and a few months before that handling cases in the crucible of Milwaukee's misdemeanor domestic violence court as a law student, I've spent eight years in criminal court. The penalties generally don't change much from year to year, the range of crimes charged is pretty standard, and often the defenses ("I wasn't really that drunk." "I never touched her." "It must have been someone else.") sound depressingly familiar.

And yet I am still awestruck, profoundly and repeatedly, by the inherent power of the criminal justice system to alter and affect people's lives, to hold bad folks accountable for their actions, to give others a second chance, to tear families apart to ensure the safety of the entire community or a single child, to shed grace on the repentant.

I remember what I felt when I first walked up to the Milwaukee County courthouse, still a student, still even newer than "wet behind the ears." The building was enormous, on the scale and style of a Greek temple, a soaring monument of granite and marble, with words like "law" and "justice" chiseled above the entrances. The language of the law was formal and difficult for the casual observer to grasp, the courtrooms guarded by armed bailiffs, the pace of the misdemeanor courts at times blinding. All in all it was majestic, monolithic, imposing, not a little terrifying. It was a lot to take in.

But later, little by little, once I'd absorbed the formalities of the process, the human costs and victories began to surface.

Forget about what you see on TV law shows. By the time a criminal case reaches the courtroom, there are no clear-cut "winners," no matter who prevails at the end. Something bad has been done and no matter what the verdict, the crime victim will not be made whole, nor the crime undone, nor any of the participants left untarnished by the experience.

And yet, small victories still flourish like wildflowers in sidewalk cracks, reminders that the human spirit is never static. The young woman, shoved into a plate glass store window by the father of her handicapped son as she pushed him in a stroller, who came to court on the day of trial, despite the defendant's cocky predictions that she wouldn't show. When he saw her, he took the deal. The repeat domestic abuser who, after his attorney pled for leniency at sentencing, told the judge "your Honor, I was eleven years old the first time I hit a woman. Do what you think you have to, because this has to stop." The twenty-year-old man seeking to have his juvenile felony conviction and firearm ban amended to misdemeanor status so that he—now a new father—could join the military, straighten up and fly right. The list of the lives we touch is endless as we wield the discretion our positions demand, and make the arguments we believe the ends of justice require.

Another Monday is just around the corner, and the DA's office will be open for business at 8:00 a.m. The only thing I'll know for certain as I flip the lights on in my office when I get there is that whatever the new day brings, this job will never end … and I will never, ever be bored.

Turbo Dating—a year in review

I'm getting really tired of reading "bad date" stories. It seems like every woman's magazine, every newspaper, every "lifestyle" website has an article about memorably awful encounters, particularly for single women over thirty-five. Moaning artfully about meeting Mr. Wrong has turned into a cottage industry.

The stories themselves are uniformly arch, and funny, and full of razor sharp detail from the gleam on the rim of a martini glass in flickering candlelight to the click of a date's false teeth and the barely concealed look of disappointment on a middle-aged guy who'd hoped for someone younger looking. The women in these modern dating chronicles are witty, plucky, resilient and cheerfully determined. And the tales are grounded in incompatibility and disappointment. If fairy tales end naturally in happy unions, these wickedly downbeat and sardonic narratives thrive on dissatisfaction and skepticism.

Here's a different perspective, based on what I'm now quaintly calling "the year of Turbo Dating." This would be the year of catching up I embarked on after my twenty-plus year marriage ended. In the final tally, I drank a lot of coffee, made a lot of small talk, had some bad dates, had some great dates, met some fellas who didn't make it past the "sixty second rule" and met some guys who were really wonderful. But at the end of that action- packed twelve months—including "meet 'n' greets" with about three dozen guys—I'd learned that the best and most important relationship I found was with myself.

The turbo dating year kicked off, naturally, with a divorce. I'd pulled the plug on a twenty five year marriage a month before the actual anniversary. It had been on life-support for a decade before that, though. While the viewing public was surprised, our children were not.

At the age of barely twenty four, with no dating experience to speak of behind me, I had married my first steady boyfriend. We met as he was finishing law school and I was finishing a journalism degree. Four children followed, and I immersed myself in both full-time motherhood and a freelance career as a magazine writer. Fifteen years later I broke my back in a horseback riding accident. Spending a few months in a body cast made me look at life in a very new way. Law school followed, then a career as a criminal prosecutor, and eventually the bonds of matrimony cracked and broke. Seven months later, after a civilized "collaborative divorce," I was suddenly single.

The general rule of thumb, or so I hear, is that the newly divorced should give themselves a couple of years to heal their emotional wounds before jumping into the dating pool. I, on the other hand, have always been something of a loose cannon, and so I waited all of four days after the ink was dry on the divorce decree before I signed up to try on-line dating.

It was only a few hours before someone hit on my profile and tentatively suggested getting together. At that instant I recoiled from the keyboard as it was on fire, recognizing that "jeez, I am *soooooooo* not ready for this!!" But within a few weeks, I finally took the plunge and scheduled two coffee dates for a weekend. In for a dime, in for a dollar.

Bachelor Number One turned out to be a walking object lesson for the fact that you can't tell what someone looks like in a single long shot photo. And that well-written emails can mask the fact that English is only your second language. Or third. I'm still not sure what his first language was...but we still spent an hour chatting with difficulty above the noise in a crowded coffee shop. I patted him on the shoulder as we parted company and said "I'm sure the right girl is out there for you!" and walked swiftly away...but not before he'd shared tales of his own internet dating horror stories. And left me with a piece of advice which I still consider priceless. That you can talk all you want about compatibility points and shared interests and matching core values... but what it really still all comes down to is "chemistry." How you answer the question, "do you want to get closer to this person?" I moved that thought to the back of my mind and set out to meet Bachelor Number Two.

This turned out to be a good looking, articulate accountant who owned a sailboat. My passion for my work as a prosecutor appeared to captivate him, and an hour of animated conversation flew by. He asked me out again, this time to dinner at a romantic lakefront restaurant. He cleaned up quite nicely. So did I. Drinks, dinner, dress-up clothes instead of jeans and sweats, a little smooching in the parking lot before parting...I couldn't have asked for a better first "real date" to start me off. A third date, at an art museum, was calendared in. And halfway through it I had one of those "eureka moments" cartoonists illustrate with light bulbs floating overhead. I realized we didn't get excited about any of the same stuff. And worse, I was dialing down my enthusiasm to match his cynicism and malaise. I think he felt it too. A brisk hug and a peck in parting in the museum parking lot, and we both drove away and never looked back. The adventure continued, and so did the education of Mary.

I kept my dating life under the radar from my children for a very long time, but regaled my girlfriends at work with tales from the front. And the theme that always floated to the top was that with every conversation, with every meeting, with every disappointment or pleasant surprise, I came away knowing a little more about myself. I was finally asking myself the questions I would have asked at the age of twenty if I'd had a social life back then. Preconceptions went right out the window as my coffee intake increased. Well *I thought I liked that*...but maybe not as much as I expected. Gee, *didn't know I liked that in a man!* Who knew? Hmmm...guess *I don't really like that after all*. And so it went.

Even the few memorably bad experiences taught me something. Such as...it's okay to be impatient and even aggravated. One evening found me sharing drinks and appetizers with a good looking guy who even described himself as an "angry white male." After his first lengthy rant—about the press and its "contempt for the military"—I found myself wondering if I'd have the guts to slap a twenty on the counter and just walk out. I didn't, and an excruciating evening ground on until his second rant—this time about illegal immigration—ran its course. As I drove home forty miles in the dark, I thought ruefully, "and I skipped sitting home in my pajamas and watching '*Medium*' for this??" Next time, I vowed, I'd be quicker to leave and cut my losses.

And then there were the kinder, gentler encounters. A guy who showed up nervously with a bouquet of flowers to meet me for the first time. Turns out it was his first date in the year that had followed his divorce, and he was scared to death to start testing the waters. There was the blue-collar guy who drove a cement truck most of the year, and a snow plow in the winter months. He was cute and funny and wore a diamond earring, and while we didn't technically call all the hanging out that we did actual "dating," we laughed and called and talked about life and politics for months, did stuff, flew a kite into a tree, met for dinner when I was passing by. For a long time he was my "go to" guy for answers to all the manly questions I knew nothing about, such as how to use my new cordless drill and how to maintain the water heater. I told him that in a blizzard, given a choice between Brad Pitt coming up the driveway on a white horse with a dozen roses and the guy with a snowplow, every woman I know would pick the guy with the plow, feeling like the cavalry had arrived for a rescue. He liked that image a lot.

Then there was the draftsman who, when I warned him that some guys found dating a "chick with a badge" a bit scary, showed up for coffee sporting a toy badge of his own pinned to his flannel shirt. I felt charmed right out of my socks.

There was a perfectly wonderful widower in the mix, too. Our e-mails were great. Our phone calls were great. The two-hour brunch we shared as a first date was great, and we left the restaurant pleasantly committed to finding time for a second. But by the end of the day, we had both agreed to call it off. On the long drive home, I'd realized that his two little boys really needed a mother figure in their lives… and after raising four kids already, it wasn't going to be me. And he'd noticed me unconsciously flinch when he brought out the pictures of his young sons, and realized that some gulfs can't be bridged. And so I learned that sometimes you have to be a grownup right out of the gate, even when it hurts.

I kept a general rule of not dating anyone farther away than 75 miles, but even that rule was meant to be broken. After months of charming and intriguing emails and phone conversations with a wildlife artist in another state, we finally agreed to meet half way to go birdwatching. We rendezvoused one morning at a wildlife refuge, with the goal of searching for whooping cranes. He turned out to be a little bit older looking than his picture, but he was still craggily handsome in a self-assured, outdoorsy way. I don't think I passed *his* sixty second rule. But we still spent a glorious day outdoors, wrapped in sunlight and soft breezes, trading stories of life and children and authorities flaunted and obstacles overcome. I'll never forget staring, awestruck, at a quartet of juvenile bald eagles as they playfully soared and swooped together, snatching fish with their talons from the water below and then dive bombing each other to get the others' prize. And at the end of the day, after hours of looking, we found a whooping crane, in splendid closeup, after all.

An evening I spent with a former military pilot changed me irrevocably. He still flew on occasion, but had recently found himself grounded because of high blood pressure. This date was literally a "one night wonder." We talked, we laughed, we teased, we flirted, we ate, we drank…and then we took in a movie so the evening could stretch even longer. We shared about our kids, our lives, our families, our marriages, our disappointments, our joys. And then he called it quits the next day by email. Go figure.

But the encounter had a profound effect on me in ways neither of us could have ever predicted. For years I have been a white-knuckle flyer. The older I got, the more afraid I became of flying. Shortly before the pilot and I met, in fact, I'd traveled to Germany to visit my son who was there as a foreign exchange student. And it was only the strength of maternal affection that got me on that plane, terror in my heart and dread in the pit of my stomach. Now I was in a plane again on the tarmac, this time flying to Phoenix to visit a friend from college. And as I sat, again terrified, in my window seat, I made a deliberate choice to try to see the act of flying through his eyes. Not as something to be endured and steeled against, but as a joy and a release. To trust the technology as proven, to embrace the thrust of liftoff , to see open horizon as something as inviting and welcoming and liberating as he did.

It worked. Flying hasn't been the same for me since.

After a year of this, I figured it was finally about time to scale back and take stock. The year had been interesting, but it had been exhausting too. One memorable weekend saw me meet up with four guys in three days…or was it three guys in four days? Details are fuzzy in a whirlwind. With only four days left on my Match.com membership, I spent an evening combing through photos and profiles, just checking for the last time whether there was anyone interesting I'd somehow missed. I came up with a half dozen possibilities. Three wrote back. One was a professional sports photographer who was smart, and cute, and so much of a rolling stone we could never agree on a good time to meet. One was "Prince Charming" by email, and equally charming by telephone…and just didn't hit the right notes in person.

I decided to break the mold with the third one, and after a flurry of emails and some phone calls, I suggested skipping the traditional "coffee date" and meeting instead at a movie theater. He was there on time, and seemed nice and cautiously friendly. We got our popcorn and sodas, settled into our seats, and waited for the commercials to end. As the start of the movie approached, I turned to him and announced that now was as good a time as any to fess up to the couple of little white lies I'd told in my online profile.

He looked at my with a skeptical squint. First, I confessed, I wasn't 48 as I'd claimed in my profile, but in fact was 50. He looked straight ahead again and nodded, then asked "and what's the other one?"

"Well," I replied, "I'm not slender either."

In profile, I could see the steady, somber features of his face instantly split wide open with a grin and he started to laugh. And as the lights dimmed and the opening credits came on, I settled comfortably back in my velvet seat and smiled, thinking, "I've got a really good feeling about this!"

I still do.

A Little Clutter Please!

The first sign that anyone had arrived out of the blue was the vigorous and enthusiastic barking of Bandit, the chocolate Lab.

Then there was the slam of a car door, the turn of the front door handle, and my "grand pug" came barreling up the stairs, followed by my younger daughter.

"Hi Mom," she smiled as she mustered her way through a pair of wagging tails and canine howdy-dos. "I just stopped in for a little while to clean up my room. We're having a rummage sale tomorrow."

Then she disappeared downstairs to what has officially been her bedroom for the past twenty four years, and I stood at the top of the stairs, feeling my moorings start to loosen and my world start to pitch. Who knew that the idea of a bedroom getting straightened up could bring such a sudden feeling of mourning?

I've been adjusting to a lot lately, and thought I was doing fine. My older daughter is getting married in a month and a half, my older son is spending his summer living on campus instead of at home, and my younger daughter is moving eight hundred miles away to grad school in two weeks. As they say, denial is not just a river in Egypt.

I've been grumbling about the state of that particular bedroom for years. Impassable, impossible, ridiculous, I've used many words with four-syllables to describe its state of perpetual disarray. There were little girl things in abundance at first, then high school things—gym socks, sports awards, photos, the leaf litter of price tags and shopping bags and candles and scrunchies and cast-off ribbons and bows. Then, after the start of college and a multitude of art classes, it became also a repository of **objets d'art** as well. Paintings on canvas, three-dimensional fabric creations, collages, sculptures. The room stood in perpetual gloom because the route across its length to get to the window was a minefield too full of hazards to think of crossing to throw open the shade.

I'll be the first to admit that the apple hasn't fallen far from the tree. I don't have filing systems, I have "piling" systems. The only things I can find for certain in my house are my cell phone, my car keys, and clean underwear. Everything else is up for grabs, dropped on the first convenient square of a few clean inches…or lacking that, on top of other stacks of stuff. Cleaning out my closets just after New Years so that the carpet layers could do their thing in the two back bedrooms was a Herculean effort that took days. And some of the stuff still hasn't moved back. I know that when I finally reach the "bottom of the barrel" in the biggest laundry basket downstairs, I'll have to do something with the set of furry grey doggie ears I made for her dance recital costume when she was three. They're still there.

But still, I thought optimistically as I periodically surveyed my daughter's nesting place, some day, the clutter would be cleared and I could put the bedroom to use as a guest room once in a while. The thought filled me with hope.

And then she showed up to clean it up, less than a month before the cross-country move, and it suddenly didn't feel so good. I busied myself in the kitchen while she worked downstairs, getting ready for the upcoming graduation/bon voyage party I'd planned as a send-off. I finally carried some laundry downstairs as an excuse to visit and see how she was doing.

She sat cross-legged on the floor, sorting, keeping, throwing out. Sunlight flooded the room through the window for the first time in recent memory, and I could see large patches of the pink carpet reemerge, clutter free. The pastel wallpaper that I'd hung nearly two decades earlier—vertical stripes of pink ribbons and bows, topped with hand-cut scallops of matching blooms against a cream background— shone softly in the afternoon light. She smiled brightly at her progress. My heart sank.

Eventually she declared herself done, loaded the pug and the items for the rummage sale in her car, and we met up for sub sandwiches with her dad and her brother before she left town. There were hugs and kisses and promises to "see you soon!"

I went to the store and drove back to the house alone, trekked down to the lower floor, opened the bedroom door. Sunlight still streamed through the window, while the breeze outside tossed the coneflowers and daylilies in the garden beyond. The room looked more than moderately useable. A few bags needed to be dragged out to the trash, but the bed was clear, as was most of the floor. I took the hit, shrugged, and closed the door behind me.

I moped acutely for the next couple of days. Then my ex-husband called unexpectedly on his way back from her student apartment. He was bringing her bed back to town and needed a place to put it until the last kid might need it for college. Did we possibly have the space in her bedroom?

Sure, I replied, and I scrambled quickly to move dresser and chair, hamper and trash bags from half of the room, and to vacuum the dusty carpet before he showed up. My single goal was to clear enough floor space to stand a queen sized mattress, spring and bed frame on end, and I piled anything in my way back on the bed indiscriminately. More had been left behind than I'd originally thought, and the bedspread was soon invisible once more under sheaves of paper, old cosmetics and empty cardboard boxes waiting to be recycled.

The bed and frame were moved in without a hitch, and when all was settled, I stood back and took inventory. The extra bed leaning against the wall dominated the landscape like a sore thumb, but what I saw made me smile. The room once again looked like a hurricane had gone through it. And once more, I had a job to look forward to doing.

Love in Wood and Wax

The words that made my heart pleasantly leap, not to mention my adrenaline surge, weren't "I love you." They were something more along the lines of "Watch it, she's coming down!"

I loosened the tension on the nylon rope I'd been pulling on, and made it a priority to get out of the way of the forty food dead tree falling into the front yard. The man who inhabits a lot of acreage in my heart had just notched the tree with his chain saw, and after a few more hours of hard and dirty work (mostly his but I kept up my end by dragging shards and broken branches to the "burn pile") it would be turned into firewood to keep me warm the next winter.

My heart glowed…and not just because I was standing next to a bonfire.

I laugh these days at how my definition of romance has changed since I was in my twenties, and what meets the test for a token of affection.

Back in the day long ago when I knew much less about what I didn't know, the language of love followed a standard script, and the symbols were equally standard issue. Flowers, of course. Candy, of course. Jewelry was always appreciated. Perfume…well that was more an individual choice, but it was the thought that counted. Oh, and don't forget dinner and a movie. The fancier and more expensive the restaurant, the bigger the thrill.

That was quite a while ago. Going off script has been so liberating!

The man in my life and I tally three ex-spouses and five kids between us, along with a cat and a dog (both mine), and three small fish that live in a tiny aquarium on his kitchen stove island. There are jobs, and bills, and responsibilities, and run-of-the-mill irritations, and heartaches we could have never imagined when we were walking out the high school door in our caps and gowns.

But along the way, we learned to see ordinary things with new eyes, and feel much the richer for it.

That lesson hit me with the force of a hammer one day last summer. My new subcompact car was still as shiny as a new penny when I was informed by my love that according to the manly code of car maintenance, it needed to be properly polished and waxed. I arched one eyebrow, but picked up a wet sponge and started slinging suds without demur. This is a man who owns not only his own buffer, he owns two.

Hours later, as midnight approached, he ruefully concluded that we'd bitten off more than we could properly chew for the evening, and handed me the keys to his F-150 for the drive to work the next day. He'd have the job finished by next evening, he thought.

When I drove back to his place a couple of days later, he was just finishing up. Even from a distance he looked exhausted. My approach was masked by the whirr of the shop vac as he whisked the last infinitesimal bits of dust from the car's interior. I stared at the car, absolutely stunned. It gleamed like a sapphire in the sun, and I could see the knife-edged reflection of overhanging branches and the subtle shading of clouds above in its mirror finish. The car hadn't looked nearly this good when I drove it away from the showroom. I could put makeup on in its refl ection.

I couldn't have been more moved if he'd surprised me with a truckload of orchids and a pair of tickets to Hawaii. And therein was an awakening.

We don't feel compelled to follow much of the old script anymore. Dinner and a movie is often chicken breast or pork tenderloin perfectly grilled over charcoal in his back yard or mine, followed by a movie on DVD. Sometimes we go lowbrow, sometimes we shoot for an Oscar winner, and half the time we just fall asleep on the sofa halfway through the movie, too tired from the rest of the week to keep our eyes open past eleven.

I watch a lot more fireflies in the evening. Viewed from the edge of the woods as twilight comes, they twinkle and gleam like sparkling gems on a dark sea, and there's a sense of mystery and surprise with the firing of every tiny light.

I get flowers often, cut from his garden, and they always make me smile. But even more, every day I step out into rose gardens flanking the front door that he planted last year when we were first starting to date. And as I walk along an Arizona sandstone footpath leading me through coneflowers and delphiniums and coreopsis and daylilies that replaced a field of crushed rock and plastic, remembering a shared crucible of heat and dirt and sweat and shredded cedar and anticipation, I think every day, "this is the garden that love built."

This year, I don't know if I'll be getting a box of fancy chocolates for Sweetest Day.

But I'm pretty sure that either in my fireplace or in a bonfire in the yard, we'll be burning some of that firewood we cut and stacked, watching the flames dance and the sparks float upwards in the dark. And somehow that seems so much sweeter.

On the road again

Whoever said "a journey of a thousand miles starts with a single step" must have been an ad man.

"A single step" **MY ASS** I grumbled to myself as I tried to remember to water the flowers off the kitchen, find the bottom half of my swimsuit, clean and pack the binoculars, locate a clean nightgown, pour enough cat food into a roasting pan that Smokey wouldn't starve to death, leave the toilet seat up in case I forgot to fill the water dish.

I stashed my son and dog with my ex-husband, arranged for the mail to be picked up, alerted the rest of the kids by email as to their mother's whereabouts with a maternal bulletin featuring a string of words they had surely never imagined assembled in sequence in the English language: *your mother is going to Florida for spring break*. Reassured the elderly parents, checked into the car insurance, raided the ATM for vacation cash, eviscerated the purse to lighten the load. Photocopied the major charge cards in case the purse got lifted when I wasn't looking.

The problem with that whole "single step" imagery is that it conjures up a zen-like focus, a deliberate, decisive, methodical advance toward a far-off goal. A rational moving forward, one step at a time. Reality is more like one step up, two steps back, a little shuffle sideways...and then do the Chicken Dance.

This trip was, in fact, a journey of a thousand miles, maybe a little more. It was a mad dash to the Gulf Coast, spawned by the absolute desperation of living through a cold and snowy Midwestern winter that seemed it would never end. The plan was simple—drive south from Wisconsin, meet up in Peoria, Illinois with my friend Kristin who was driving in from her home in Iowa, and keep driving south until we hit the first beach we saw on the Gulf of Mexico. Bask like lizards in the sun for two days, then turn around and head home.

Pretty basic. But impossible to definitively make out that "single step" thing. Frenzy was more accurate. Herding cats absolutely nails it.

This is how, as F. Scott Fitzgerald once noted, the very rich are different from you and me. They've got minions to do the heavy lifting for them. Do you think Bill Gates ever frets that he hasn't properly packed his travel-sized toothpaste in a quart-sized ziplock bag prior to boarding his private jet? Do you think Angelina Jolie wakes up at three in the morning thinking that she'd better top off the litter box with another inch of Tidy Cats before she leaves? Does Warren Buffett take the time to ask his neighbors to "keep an eye on the place"? Ha ha ha!!!

In some ways, the adventure began an entire day before, with a trip to pick up the rental car at a Sheraton hotel thirty miles away from home, a detour to my boyfriend's house to stash my own car in his garage for safekeeping while I was gone, and an intervening Bruce Springsteen concert in the eighteen hours between renting the vacation car and actually nosing it south out of my driveway, the front door locked behind me and the porch light on. I'd bought those tickets months before, while there was still warmth in the autumn air, and there was no way I was missing that concert. Had it not been for Bruce, the beach basking time could have been extended to three days or four. What a dilemma!

And in and around the car rental were squeezed comparison shopping for hotel rooms on the internet, the stop at the local AAA office for maps and travel books, runs for sunscreen and prescriptions, reorganizing my collection of CDs for some proper "traveling music," putting Jimmy Buffett and the Beach Boys in easy reach. I'll never be able to remember the half of it, just the image of a tidal wave of persnickety details that felt like death by a thousand cuts.

When, against all odds and timing, I was finally ready to leave and was only an hour behind schedule, I nosed the car north, not south.

In my rearview mirror was a driveway coated with sleet from the night before, and the grass still held a heavy frosting of ice. Fog swirled around the car as drove a familiar path toward town, to the drive-thru at Starbucks. I placed my order, inching forward, making last minute adjustments to the collection of CDs in the rack on the visor. Double checked that the driving directions to Peoria were within arm's reach.

The magic Plexiglas portal above me opened, money changed hands, and finally a tall soy mocha with whipped cream made its way into my car. The familiar aroma permeated the air around me. I relaxed instantly as the hot liquid hit my throat and my tastebuds reveled in the familiar and comforting. I pulled out of the parking lot, and eased the rental car toward the expressway ramp.

The journey of a thousand miles had finally started. Everything else was prologue.

Thelma and Louise on spring break

One state west, in Missouri, the weather system we were passing through had turned absolutely deadly. Kristin and I blithely drove south, favorite CDs playing on the stereo system and a can of Diet Coke apiece. More than a dozen people had died as a result of the storms we drove through that day in Missouri, Kentucky and southern Illinois.

But at the time, all we knew was that the windshield wipers kept going "bumpety, bumpety, bumpety" every time they dragged across the glass for nine hours straight, the rental car's steering had a definite "float" to it, especially in the wind, and the water in the drainage channels beside the two-lane road in southern Illinois was getting a wee bit high.

The Dairy Queen sign where we stopped to freshen up looked like it would be under water soon. Raindrops broke the surface of the gleaming black pool that surrounded it, lights from a nearby gas station shimmering off the rising water. At the rate we were going, we were never going to make it to our motel in Montgomery, Alabama before three a.m. We settled on looking for a cheap room in Birmingham, found a double on our third try after midnight.

Welcome to spring break. Or "Girls Gone Mild."

The first day of midlife adventure had started off with not much to recommend it. Thick, cottony fog cloaked most of the first leg of my trip from Wisconsin to Peoria, Illinois, where my law school buddy Kristin and I had agreed to meet to carpool for the rest of this midlife adventure. The fog had slowed me by about an hour, and the fact that I didn't take five extra minutes to map the route to the Peoria airport before leaving added another. Really, I'd thought smugly, how hard could it be to find an airport in Peoria? For that matter, how big could Peoria really be? A lot bigger than I thought, as it turned out, and the kindness of strangers is no substitute for a map and a set of driving directions for dummies.

No matter, Kristin and I were on a road trip for the history books, and we were undeterred. Sanity and good sense had nothing to do with it. We were fed up with winter, pure and simple, and we were goin' south.

Winter had been long and ghastly in our neck of the woods, which roughly sketched would be a swath across Iowa, Minnesota, Illinois and Wisconsin. Snowstorm after snowstorm. School cancellation after school cancellation. Temperatures below zero. Days that I dutifully drove the fifty miles to work only to desperately wish, halfway there and fishtailing on snow-covered roads, that I'd stayed safely home in bed.

And the winds and the grey skies just kept coming. It felt, deep down and for the first time that I could remember, like I would never see spring or green grass again. Like I was living in the ice cap of the Arctic Circle, and flowers were something to be admired only in catalogs, grown by happy shirt-sleeved gardeners in tropical warm, sunny places thousands of miles south. By early March something in me had snapped and I became a desperate woman. Apparently the malaise was catchy, because Kristin and I charged off the blocks only four days after she—living a good six hours away in Iowa—sold her husband on the idea that she really needed a winter break too, and that he and their two daughters could spare her attentions for a few days.

The plan was simple—drive straight south until we hit the Gulf of Mexico, and stop at the first beach we saw. And setting aside the first day and a half of driving through steady rain, it actually worked. About the time we got sixty miles from Gulf Shores, Alabama, the clouds finally parted, the sun came out, and we saw blue skies above. And sure enough, when we finally ran out of highway, the road ended in a large paved public parking lot at the edge of a pure, white sand beach, with enormous breakers kicking up spray a few hundred feet out. We locked the car, rolled up our pants, and happily waded in. We'd made it.

The trip was especially sweet when I thought back to my college years and realized I'd never properly been on "spring break" before. While friends and classmates were piling on to buses and into cars and speeding south in the middle of March, I was usually working. And somehow, multiple instances of herding four kids and a spouse and six pieces of luggage and a half suitcase full of Easter chocolate and bunny bags and plastic Easter grass hidden under socks and a nightgown for a family vacation in a condo on the Georgia coast didn't quite qualify.

The words "spring break" just had a connotation of more carefree abandon, of caution to the wind, of randomness and adventure and opportunity and the Great Unknown. Of course, they also conjured up popular visions of "Girls Gone Wild" and drunken revelry and bikini-ready hardbodies oiled up and ready for Mai Tais and short-lived romance. But hey, we had to start somewhere.

There are advantages to doing some things when you're older. Sometimes it's simply that you know, starting out, that your friendship is strong enough to survive a cramped, muscle-screaming drive of twelve hundred miles in two days in a compact car. In our case, the catching up we did during the drive was half the adventure. We'd weathered law school together, with all its paranoia and all-the-eggs-in-one-basket semester exams and anxiety and pressure and competition and chocolate cravings. Since graduating Kristin and her family had moved twice, I'd gotten divorced and adjusted to all that that big change brings, and between the two of us, a full fifty percent of our children had weathered serious health crises resulting in major surgery. Not to take anything away from the incredible courage and grace and resilience of our kids in dealing with these horribly inequitable turns of chance…but that kind of misfortune gives two mothers a lot to talk about as the miles roll by.

Another advantage to being…say, over thirty…is that you don't feel you've got to reinvent the wheel and discover everything for yourself to make lasting memories. I'd picked Gulf Shores as a destination because a clerk at the courthouse suggested that it would be a nice place to visit, and two minutes on the internet later that night had me sold.

Walking the beach that first evening, we struck up a conversation with a local and asked him where a good restaurant serving seafood might be found. He pointed us up the street to a place with a full parking lot and a dolphin statue outside, and boy, was he right!

The next morning, with a full day of beach-going to make the most of, I wound up sharing breakfast with an elderly gentleman from Illinois who shanghaied me in the parking lot while Kristin—never a "morning person"—slept in, and directed me to the tourist welcome center I'd blindly driven past twice in the dark the night before. Asked for the best, quietest beach around, the clerk at the welcome center pointed us to Cotton Bayou beach a few miles down the coast, her personal favorite. Just to say we did, we drove past it by a few miles and into Florida looking for something better…and not finding it, turned right back. Took her advice on a seafood restaurant near the beach for dinner too, wolfing down plate after plate of seafood appetizers, selfishly foregoing entirely the niceties of a full dinner (rolls, salad, potatoes, veggies) in favor of crabmeat and shrimp and grilled tuna from start to finish. And after dinner, as we walked along the shore and watched the rising full moon shimmer over the shore, we never regretted not wasting our time looking for something better.

And the beach alone was worth it.

Pure white "sugar sand" soft and clean underfoot, the rise and fall of waves rushing in, the chorus of black-faced laughing gulls behind us, sounding like a bunch of raucous monkeys in a tree. As I walked along the water's edge, stopping to pick up the occasional small, perfect shell, I felt very much like the little girl I used to be, bent over and searching with single purpose for tiny shells along the edge of the Montrose Avenue beach in Chicago as the sun beat down on my shoulders.

Anne Morrow Lindbergh had it exactly right in her book of heartfelt essays, "Gift from the Sea," when she wrote that "the beach is not the place to work; to read, write or think." I have forgotten that many times over the years, bringing notebooks and pens and lists and good intentions to the shore as she once had, expecting to find the inspiration to write, only to find myself mesmerized by the sound of the waves and the wind. For me, it's like listening to the world breathe. Even this time, I had efficiently packed both a book and a magazine in my tote bag—"Angels and Demons" by Dan Brown and the latest Oprah magazine, you couldn't ask for better, less demanding beach reading than that—and still found myself hypnotized by my surroundings. Th e book and the magazine remained untouched as I stretched out full-length and dug my fingers into the warm, perfect sand surrounding me.

Instead of "accomplishing" anything, we shopped a little for souvenirs to bring home. And stretched out on the shore a lot, waking only long enough to turn over and broil our other sides. Lounging like lizards in the sun, we felt the energy of the universe permeate our frozen bone marrow and imprint our shivering psyches with memories of warmth that would last us the rest of the winter. With two blankets and plenty of sunblock, there was nothing essential that we lacked. We lunched, and breakfasted, and otherwise snacked throughout the day on seafood dip on crackers brought in a picnic cooler that also held hummus, and goat cheese, and grapes, and fancy chocolates, and unspecified beverages which may or may not have contained alcohol in violation of local ordinance.

While the signs posted at the edge of the beach all warned that alcoholic beverages were verboten, well, we were females over the age of thirty in bathing suits on a public beach, while college kids with better bodies in skimpier suits frolicked and played Frisbee and volleyball nearby. In other words, we were absolutely invisible. *A votre santé!* Having left our only bottle opener--my Swiss Army knife--back in the hotel room, Kristin laughingly drew on what she called her "sketchy past" and taught me how to open a long-necked bottle with a house key. Hey, it's never too late to learn a new social skill.

Two days at the shore passed far too quickly by any measure. We skipped a trip to a nearby outlet mall—surely a first for us—in favor of spending the last few hours on the beach. Packed up and left straight from the shore, sand still in our shoes and windows down, the sound of the waves and the laughing gulls fading behind us. The drive back was dry this time, but at two days, still far too long for anything like comfort. We split again at the Peoria airport, with a shuffle of baggage and a quick hug before resuming our last sprints back toward reality. In my case, the real world involved Easter dinner for eight at my house the next day…after a mad dash to the supermarket Easter morning for something to cook. Fifteen inches of fresh snow that fell the day we left Alabama welcomed me back as a bonus.

But I brought a piece of the shore back with me. Not just in memory, but in a few handfuls of white sand and a half dozen shells in colors of grey and white and tangerine. Dug up with my own hands from a spot right next to my beach blanket, transported inartfully in a plastic grocery bag, and encased now in a glass jar and wrapped with a ribbon the color of seafoam, a miniature version of the Gulf of Mexico sits on my desk at work, the swirls of the seashells drawing me hypnotically back to the rhythm of the shore, and reminding me daily of the value of acting on impulse once in a while.

Before I pick up another magazine or finish "Angels and Demons"…I think I'll re-read "Gift from the Sea" once more.

Emergency Makeup Kit

I've laughed over the years--and been laughed at too, usually by one man or another--at the thought that I've got what I call "emergency makeup kits" stockpiled around. They're stocked mostly with tiny makeup samples from bonus times at cosmetic counters--and bagged in one of the myriad colorful little "bonus bags" they came in.

There are emergency supplies, and then there are emergency supplies. My kids have also snickered at the size of the box full of stuff I usually keep in the back of the car simply because it's so big and ridiculously thorough. Shovel, first-aid kit, spare shoes, jacket, gloves, scarves, candles, matches, light bars...and don't forget the Swiss Army Knife sitting in the map holder. This set of gear takes up more than half the car's storage space in back.

The makeup kits are dainty by comparison, but they function as a safety net if I ever need to drop everything while grocery shopping and go meet the Queen of England. To date, I've got three. One's in a drawer in my office, one's in my locker at the Sheriff's Department next door in case I ever get motivated enough to go exercise again over the lunch hour, (ha! ha!), and one's in the glove box of my car.

I didn't foresee I was really going to need one just a few weeks ago. I hadn't gotten any calls from Buckingham Palace, and as for exercise... we'll let that one lie. But halfway through the morning at my desk I found a voicemail from my younger daughter telling me that for a bunch of reasons—none of which she was happy with—what would have been her last night at home before moving across the country was off. It hit me like a two-by-four, and it wasn't long before I was just a puddle of tears.

I'd seen her just a few days before, but had skipped a big "goodbye" because I knew I'd be seeing her, her boyfriend, the grandpug and the spare cat for an overnight in just a few days. Gave her a quick peck on the cheek, a wave and a "see you soon!" The menu was planned for her favorites, I was going to bake brownies as a surprise, you know how it goes. And now that happy evening had vanished, leaving a very big hole. A cop I work with passed by my office door just as I began to dissolve, and ended up on one knee beside me, patting my back to comfort me as I gulped out my sorrow and distress. The perfect man... but he knows who he is and so we won't embarrass him any further.

I fled the building sobbing, and drove down to the harbor nearby, where the cold wind off Lake Michigan cooled a lot of things down. A half hour of solitude and mourning later, it was finally time to get back to work. I reached in the glove box and found the makeup bag. Moisturizer, eye-liner pencil, eye shadow and brow highlighter, blush, lipstick, perfume. All in itty bitty sizes, with itty bitty applicators, along with an itty bitty mirror. I did the best I could with this Lilliputian repair kit.

But by the time I parked at the courthouse and walked back into the building to spend the rest of the afternoon in court, I had my game face on.

I could always cry it off again on the way home.

Ghosts in the Pasture

The weeds in the unused paddock grew five feet high and more, and I parted them gingerly with my hands as I walked across sandy soil to the pasture fence. There had been no equine hooves churning the ground impatiently this summer, prancing and pounding it to bare dirt as I approached for the morning turn-out. Nature abhors a vacuum, and a phantasmagorical forest of lacy and slender foliage sprang gracefully from the windswept soil, a tall, swaying barricade to be traversed before yielding the keys to memory.

I hadn't started with this goal in mind. All I set out to accomplish was three quick turns around the edge of the property at a brisk walk for some exercise. Drenching rains and pressure cooker temps had combined recently to hatch a vicious crop of mosquitoes, and venturing outside had become like armed warfare. The bugs were winning, the humans cowering behind screens and air conditioners and aerosol cans of smelly insect repellant. But the weather had turned unseasonably cold again, and the chilly morning air and a stiff wind had temporarily parted the veil of bloodsucking pests. Time to press the advantage, and make the most of a walk in the woods before it turned warm and tropic again.

I walked happily up and down the hills and along the flats, down a path overhung in places with evergreen branches and through a field of grass shot through with morning glories and milkweed. My route took me alongside the pasture where the horses had grazed for two decades. Brush had grown up along the fence line over the past few years, making the posts and woven wire now nearly invisible.

I basked in the sunlight as I walked, the wind clean and cool on my face. Not much occupied my mind but the sights and smells around me—a handful of wild mushrooms here, a discarded turkey feather there, pine cones and dead branches, a sumac leaf prematurely turning blood red in a field of green, heralding the inevitable end of summer— and the occasional thought of what new perennial or two I'd like to buy next for the fl ower beds.

But I slowed as I reached the wooden paddock fence at the end of my last lap, and stopped to look in. It was empty. The last of the horses had died the winter before. The steel water tanks lay tipped forlornly on their sides where they had rested for nearly a year, and the paddock felt strangely silent. No snorts of recognition, no hoofbeats thudding, no hearty knocks and scraping sounds as feed buckets clattered on their hooks while the two horses dove in to their twice-daily race to the bottom. It was always a competition, where the fastest eater then tried to get seconds by shouldering aside the slower gastronome.

I had never seen it like this, and I unlatched the gate. Tall grass had sprung up undisturbed around the base, and it took some tugging to dislodge. The wood had weathered to a splintered, silvery grey from years of use. I left it standing open. No need to bolt it behind me anymore, the casualness going against the grain of thirty odd years of habit in owning horses and cutting off their escape. I passed the two-sided shed in the corner of the paddock where they had weathered countless rain and snow storms, and took cover from the blazing sun on the summers' hottest days. It felt like a ghost town.

The new forest of weeds finally behind me, I struggled a bit with the heavy gate to the pasture itself. It stood in a break between lines of tall evergreens. I stepped through, into the sunlight and three acres of pasture. The grass, ungrazed and untrampled, was deeper and more lush than I had ever seen it before. The clover had long since stopped flowering, but a field of Queen Anne's lace spread across the middle. There was still a bare groove in the dirt approaching the paddock, worn by two decades of answering the call to the evening feeding at a trot or a gallop. New saplings sprang up at random, with no one left to chew them down.

I walked entirely to the far end of the pasture, something I had rarely done when Hoki and Babe were still alive. Then, my reason for being there was usually to call them in for a feeding or a rendezvous with the veterinarian or the farrier. Vaccinations, hoof trims, examinations for various troubles, there was always a faint air of urgency and impatience to calling them back to closed quarters. This time, I had the twin luxuries of time and reverie. A flock of two dozen cedar waxwings flitted from branch to branch in a dead tree as I passed underneath. I looked for the flock of wild turkeys that had often frequented the pasture, but didn't see or hear them.

Memories came back as I walked, picturesque snapshots from the past. The hard times were forgotten, nailed shut and buried. No thoughts of blizzards, rain storms, colic, middle of the night trips to freezing barns, heartbreaks, tears, and desperate measures. The only images that surfaced this day were short, and fragmented, and beautiful. Babe, the palomino, looking like an equine pin-up in a field of flowers, ears pitched forward and brown eyes wide and alert. Hoki, the buckskin, trotting gamely along on arthritic legs to answer the dinner bell, his gait the sign of an old man, but his dappled coat gold and beautiful and, until his last year, still youthful. Babe, wheeling and prancing playfully, or rolling freely in the dirt to scratch her back. Hoki, dense but utterly devoted to his female companion, master of his one-horse "herd." I finally turned back, feeling very lucky.

As I reached the paddock again, I stopped to check out the emergency fence repairs I had made a couple of years earlier. I still have the cordless drill I bought that same day, and the confidence I gained from having to put it to use. The boards I sawed and drilled and fastened still looked new. But the twine scaffolding I left hanging from one had disappeared, no doubt nesting material for some bird or mouse in the neighborhood. The pasture gate swung shut more easily this time, and I fastened it one last time out of habit. It would keep no one in or out anymore.

Then I made my way across the sand and back through the ghostly weeds, tugged the second gate firmly into place, shot the bolt home… and closed the gate on the past.

About the Author

Mary T. Wagner's *Running with Stilettos* essays have been described in terms ranging from "barbed-wire prose" to "bedtime tales for grown-ups."

An experienced journalist and prosecutor living in Wisconsin, Wagner draws on her experiences as a newspaper reporter, soccer mom, truck stop waitress, judicial clerk, office temp, radio talk show host and cocktail waitress to craft this compelling collection of ordinary moments viewed with extraordinary insight.

She counts the ability to drive a flat-bed truck, milk a cow by hand, and hit the occasional clay pigeon with a twenty-gauge among the more valuable skills that never made it into her professional resume.